W9-BYL-702

Trafalgar
The Nelson Touch

DAVID HOWARTH

PHOENIX
A Windrush Press Book

A PHOENIX PAPERBACK

First published in Great Britain in 1969
by Collins as *Trafalgar: The Nelson Touch*
This paperback edition published in 1997
by The Windrush Press

Reissued in 2003
in association with The Windrush Press
by Phoenix,
an imprint of Orion Books Ltd,
Orion House, 5 Upper St Martin's Lane,
London WC2H 9EA

Phoenix Paperbacks
Sterling Publishing Co Inc
387 Park Avenue South
New York
NY 10016-8810
USA

The Windrush Press
Windrush House
12 Adlestrop
Moreton in Marsh
Glos GL56 0YN

Copyright © 1969, 1997 by David Howarth
Published by special arrangement with Stephen Howarth,
Literary Trustee to the Estate of the late David Howarth

The right of David Howarth to be identified as the author
of this work has been asserted by him in accordance with
the Copyright, Designs and Patents Act 1988.

All rights reserved. No part of this publication may be
reproduced, stored in a retrieval system, or transmitted,
in any form or by any means, electronic, mechanical,
photocopying, recording or otherwise, without the prior
permission of the copyright owner.

A CIP catalogue record for this book
is available from the British Library.

ISBN 1 84212 717 9

Typeset at The Spartan Press Ltd,
Lymington, Hants

Printed and bound in Great Britain by
Clays Ltd, St Ives plc

256.766.0911

Porsche 1965 356c

Thomas Trissl   *1600 c Karmen Coupe*

David Howarth read physics and mathematics at Trinity College, Cambridge. After graduating he worked for John Logie Baird, the inventor of television. This led him to join the BBC in its early days where he worked, often in tandem with Richard Dimbleby, as a presenter. In the Second World War he became a war correspondent for the BBC, reporting the chaos of Dunkirk, but with the fall of France he joined the Navy and was posted to Scapa Flow. From there he came under the command of the Special Operations Service running clandestine operations between Shetland and Norway. For this he was awarded the Norwegian Cross of Freedom and was created a Knight in the Order of St Olav, 1st Class – the highest honours that Norway could bestow upon a foreigner. In peacetime David Howarth remained in Shetland where he owned and ran a boatyard which built the traditional fishing boats peculiar to the islands. It was then that he started his writing career with the publication in 1951 of *The Shetland Bus*, a book about his wartime work which became a bestseller. Later books included *Dawn of D-Day, Waterloo: A Near Run Thing, The Greek Adventure, 1066: The Year of the Conquest* and *The Voyage of the Armada*. He also wrote and presented BBC documentaries, notably a portrait of Nelson in the 'Great Britons' series and 'Graf Spee'. David Howarth died in 1991, at the age of 78.

CONTENTS

LIST OF ILLUSTRATIONS,
PLANS AND MAPS

MAPS AND PLANS

DAWN

At ten to six in the morning of the 21st of October 1805, off Cape
Trafalgar in the south of Spain, Napoleon's French and Spanish
fleet was sighted against the dawn sky, and men in the British
fleet who were not on watch swarmed up on deck to look.

It was a beautiful autumn morning, clear under a hazy sky,
with a breeze from the west-north-west so light that the sea was
scarcely ruffled. The British ships, in line ahead, were sailing
slowly north, and rolling in a long Atlantic swell. Some had
names that were famous already, and some became famous
that day: Victory, Royal Sovereign, Temeraire, Dreadnought,
Revenge, Colossus, Ajax, Euryalus, Bellerophon – twenty-seven
sail of the line in all, and four frigates. But they were a sight so
familiar that nobody spared them a glance, except the officers of
the watch on each of the quarterdecks, whose duty was to keep
their own ship in station. Everyone else watched the lightening
horizon. For more than two years of tedious patrol, summer and
winter, blockading Napoleon's ports, the horizon at every dawn
had been empty. Now, in eager anticipation, they counted the
distant enemy sail: twenty, twenty-five, thirty – thirty-three of
them, and frigates among them, a column five miles long,
standing south for the Strait of Gibraltar.

There were seventeen thousand men in the British fleet, and
no doubt there were some whose hearts sank at seeing themselves out-numbered. But if there were, they kept their feelings to
themselves. In every glimpse that still survives of that sighting at
dawn – the diaries, dispatches, letters and reminiscences – the
predominant feeling is of excitement, and pleasure at the

prospect of a fight. Telescopes were trained on the Victory, awaiting the orders of the commander-in-chief; and a few minutes after six, as soon as it was light enough for flags to be seen, Lord Nelson hoisted the first of his signals that morning: to prepare for battle, and then, in the words of the naval signal book, to bear up and sail large on the course set by the admiral. The Victory's bow began to swing, into the path of the rising sun. In each ship, the order was repeated, men heaved on the steering wheel, the huge oak tiller creaked across to port, and deckhands manned the sheets to trim the sails: and every ship, slow, ponderous and silent, altered course towards the enemy. All sail was set, and as the morning advanced and the sun grew warmer, an air that was almost festive pervaded the fleet. Bands on the poops of some of the ships played 'Rule Britannia' and 'Britons Strike Home', and were plainly heard in the ships that had no band. From time to time, captains hailed each other with megaphones, and wished each other an enemy ship in tow before the night. Small boats were launched and rowed from ship to ship, for in the breath of wind the speed of the fleet was less than a rower's pace. And down in the gloom of the gun decks men chalked defiant slogans on their guns.

The French and Spanish did not sight the British fleet until six o'clock, because the light was behind them. When they did, their feelings at the sight were different. The British felt they had caught their enemy: the French and Spanish felt they had been caught. The British never doubted Nelson would lead them to victory; but a good many of the French and Spanish suspected their own admiral of cowardice, and only hoped at the best to save their own honour in defeat. They were willing to fight, but among those who were well informed there was not much doubt of what the result would be if a battle began. The only doubt, at dawn, was whether the breeze would hold so that a battle could begin that day, and end before the night.

It held, and slowly drove forward the British fleet to its victory and tragedy. The victory under sail that afternoon established a supremacy at sea which lasted all through the age of steam and into the age of oil, until air power made sea power insufficient. But the tragedy has overshadowed the victory ever since. The death of Nelson is a very well-known story; but in the battle, and the storm which came after it, four hundred and fifty other British sailors died, and ten times as many on the other side.

This is not to say that story-telling has put the death of Nelson out of proportion. That very evening, as soon as the news of it spread through the British fleet, the elation of victory vanished in sorrow for that single man. 'My heart is rent with the most poignant grief': so Admiral Collingwood, as second in command, wrote in the official dispatch. 'Our dear Admiral Nelson is killed,' a sailor wrote home to his father; 'chaps that fought like the devil, sit down and cry like a wench.' Hardy, the robust and forthright captain of the Victory, wrote: 'It has cost the country a life that no money can replace, and one for whose death I shall for ever mourn.' 'I too have lost a friend I loved and adored,' a fellow admiral wrote. And Dr. Scott, who was Nelson's chaplain: 'When I think, setting aside his heroism, what an affectionate fascinating little fellow he was . . . I become stupid with grief for what I have lost.' To Englishmen who fought at Trafalgar, the commander they lost seemed more important than the victory they won; and looking back at the battle so long ago, nobody now can claim to say they were wrong. Their victory was unique, but so was their love of their commander: and the love was the principal cause of the victory.

Some battles can be described in isolation: their only emotions are the fear, enmity, courage, pride and ambition which everyone feels, in varying measures, if he is caught up in such events. But at Trafalgar there were other emotions. At dawn, there was the confidence on one side and the lack of it on the other: not many great battles have been fought in which one side – the outnumbered side – was perfectly sure it would win, and the other was almost sure it would lose. Then, all through the forenoon, everyone waited with nothing to do while the British fleet crept down on its enemy, and the French and Spaniards helplessly manoeuvred in the ocean swell and the meagre wind. There was plenty of time then, six hours, for every man to think over his secret fear and weigh it against the thought of what he was fighting for. Then the short shock of the battle, the cheers of victory, the sudden silence and the grief. And finally the storm which broke next day and caught the crippled ships off the shoals of a lee shore, when humanity and seamanship united everyone, and enemies struggled to save each others' lives.

All these emotions grew from events that had gone before the battle; and so, to understand the men who fought at Trafalgar, one has to look back before it. One has to feel the fear of invasion in England and the boredom of blockading Napoleon's ports; and on the French and Spanish side the frustration of manning a fleet which for month after month was unable to put to sea. And of course one has also to recollect, so far as one can, the lost art of sailing and fighting square-rigged ships, and know something of the whims and personalities of men on both sides who sailed them on that day in 1805.

BLOCKADE

The victory was not really won that afternoon: it had already been won. In the two years before it, the British fleet had performed the greatest sustained and communal feat of seamanship there has ever been, or ever will be; and that had defeated Napoleon's navy without a single shot. Trafalgar itself was like the knock-out blow at the end of a prize-fight: one of the fighters had won all the previous rounds on points, and the other was worn out by trying to dodge the punches. And yet, although the result of the battle could be foreseen, no man on either side could foresee his own fate: would he survive, and would his ship survive? The danger was as great as in any other naval battle, and so were the fear, excitement and suspense.

Two years before, the British fleet had put to sea with the strongest motive for fighting that anyone can have – to protect his own home from invasion. At that time, even the stupidest sailor knew what the fleet had to do. Napoleon's army was ready and waiting to cross the Channel and land on the coast of England. He had an enormous flotilla of boats, equipped to bring it across. There was only one thing he lacked. He had to bring his fleet into the Channel, if only for a day or two, to protect the boats and the army while they crossed. This fleet was scattered in harbours round the coast of France, and later round the coast of Spain – in Toulon and Cartagena in the Mediterranean, and Cadiz, Vigo, Ferrol, Rochefort and Brest in the Atlantic. If they had put to sea, they might have combined in a single fleet that was strong enough to force its way up Channel. So the British fleet was stationed to lie in wait off each of the ports, to stop the enemy coming out or fight them if they tried.

In 1805 this simple strategic situation was still exactly the same. But whatever heroic feeling the British sailors had started with, the years at sea, cruising endlessly off the enemy ports, cut off from the rest of the world, had worn it down. They had gone to sea to fight, but the enemy would not fight. Blockading had been a dreary anti-climax, and did not seem to them a great achievement. That morning off Cadiz, they had almost forgotten why they had to beat the French, down there in the south of

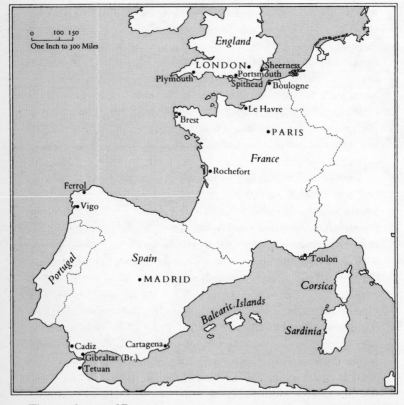

The naval ports of Europe

Spain so far from home. They had a vague hope of glory, and a definite hope of prize money, and they passionately wanted a victory which would lead to peace – but peace, to most of them, no longer meant anything so grand as the freedom of England or the safety of their families. It mainly meant the end of a boring duty. The senior officers still had the real objective in mind, but even they were sick of cruising. Nelson had had enough of it, and had told the Prime Minister so. Admiral Collingwood was worn out by it, and longed to go ashore and settle down. So did every captain whose letters have been preserved. And down on the gun decks, among the inarticulate men for whom one sea, one day or one coast was exactly like any other, the boredom must have been even more profound. They wanted to fight because they wanted to get it over and go home: a few hours' bloody battle seemed far more attractive than another winter at sea.

Something like forty or fifty thousand men must have been at sea in the blockade, but none of them wrote very much about it: perhaps none of them ever imagined that anyone else would be interested in what seemed to them so tedious. The most evocative glimpse of it was given by a boy named Bernard Coleridge. His ship was blockading Brest, and he was 11 years old, and he wrote to his father and mother: 'Indeed we live on beef which has been ten or eleven years in corn and on biscuit which quite makes your throat cold in eating it owing to the maggots which are very cold when you eat them, like calves-foot jelly or blomonge being very fat indeed. Indeed, I do like this life very much, but I cannot help laughing heartily when I think of sculling about the old cyder-tub in the pond, and Mary Anne Cosserat capsizing into the pond just by the mulberry bush. I often think what I would give for two or three quarendons off the tree on the lawn with their rosy cheeks! We drink water of the colour of the bark of a pear-tree with plenty of little maggots and weavils in it and wine which is exactly like bullock's blood and sawdust mixed together. I hope I shall not learn to swear, and by God's assistance I hope I shall not.'

Bernard Coleridge was killed when he was 14: he fell out of the rigging. But he had managed to put into words three things that older men felt strongly too: homesickness, discomfort – and yet, in spite of everything, a stubborn liking for the life a sailor led.

It is only through scraps like this that anyone can describe the blockade – the limbo from which the British sailors emerged on Trafalgar day. About sixty ships-of-the-line had maintained it, each of sixty-four to a hundred guns. Off Brest, in the Bay of Biscay and the western approaches to the English Channel, they were commanded by Admiral Cornwallis; in the Mediterranean, by Admiral Nelson. Frigates, which were smaller, faster and more manoeuvrable, attended them for observation and communication, together with a few brigs, sloops and schooners, which were smaller still.

Almost all sailing ships are beautiful, being blends of art and science, and one cannot quite avoid a romantic picture of those ships, investing them on their ceaseless watch with qualities of gallantry and splendour. But remembering their beauty, it is easy to forget their other qualities. The beauty of a ship is external, and mostly fortuitous: the functional shape of a hull, and the natural shape of a sail filled with wind, make spacious curves which please the human eye. The naval ships of Nelson's time had less beauty of line than many others: they were bluff, square, solid, built for seaworthiness and fighting strength. They had the rough beauty of master-craftsmanship and fitness for their purpose, and no doubt their size, slowness and silence gave them an air of stateliness when they were under way. But people who saw them seldom made any comment on it, and connoisseurs of that era preferred the work of French and Spanish builders. Not many artists who painted them had also lived in them. People who had knew only too well that they were damp, insanitary and overcrowded, with no provision whatever, except in the officers' cabins, for any physical comfort. Every description of them ought to evoke a smell – of tar, bilge water, sodden timber, old salt meat, rum, gunpowder and closely packed human bodies.

A ship-of-the-line was upwards of 200 feet in length and 50 in beam, and it carried six to eight hundred men. It was a self-sufficient world of its own. It had an independence which vanished when steam began, because steamships needed fuel – an independence which perhaps has been regained with atomic power. Nelson's ships could stay at sea as long as the strength of their officers and men would let them: all they needed, once in three months or so, was food and water from supply ships or from boats in the outer roadstead of a port – and once in a matter of years a dock to scrape the weed and barnacles off their bottoms. And they did stay at sea, scarcely touching the land, summer and winter, calm and storm, in heat and bitter cold. Nelson, on the blockade, was two years without setting foot off the decks of the Victory. Few of the crew had been ashore in that time, and those few had only been to fill water-casks at streams in Sardinia or perhaps to take beef on board in Tetuan. And Collingwood had once kept the sea for twenty-two continuous months without ever dropping anchor.

For these long voyages, which had no destination and no end in sight, the crews were turned in on themselves. From each other they had no privacy whatever, but from the outside world they suffered the isolation of hermits. They received their orders from the flags the admiral hoisted. Sometimes they came within hailing distance of another ship. In calm weather, captains were rowed from ship to ship, and the boats' crews had a chance to hear the gossip of the fleet. But news of events in the world only reached them as distant rumours long out of date, and news of home was rare, especially on the Mediterranean station. A doctor named Leonard Gillespie joined the Victory off Sardinia on January 2nd, 1805. On the 7th he dutifully began a letter to his sister. But it was March 16th before a ship left the fleet to sail for England and gave him a chance to send his letter home – and it would have taken another month on the way. With the best of luck, it might have been midsummer before he could look for an answer.

Nelson's sailors therefore wrote far fewer letters home than

Wellington's soldiers. They had nothing to write about, except on days like Trafalgar. Soldiers saw foreign places and met strange people, and their life was something anyone at home could comprehend. But sailors saw nobody but their shipmates, and nothing but the sea and other ships, and distant shores; and their work and daily life could only be described in sailor's language. Perhaps they sometimes found a pen and paper, and a corner of a bench to put the paper on, and then found their minds a blank at the problem of telling land-lubberly relations what they were doing. At all events, only the most literate of them, with the strongest family ties, wrote letters at all, or hoped to receive them. The majority lost all touch with their families while they were at sea. Whether they liked it or not, the ship became the only home they had.

These sailors of Nelson's time are distinctive figures in English social history, but since they so seldom put a pen to paper, hardly anything is known about them as individual men. In their lifetimes they were an amorphous, anonymous mass of humanity, and so they must always remain, except in fiction. Beside the few who wrote letters, half a dozen or so out of all the thousands wrote reminiscences; but only one of those fought at Trafalgar. Many admirals and captains wrote obliquely about the seamen – the people, as they sometimes called them – but theirs was a special view, and possibly prejudiced. Admiralty Orders and manuals of seamanship give some factual clues to their daily lives, and the logs of the ships tell a bare story of where they went and what they did. But because authentic sources are so sparse, two contradictory portraits of the sailors have persisted: at one extreme, the Jolly Jack Tars, brave, patriotic and devil-may-care; and at the other, the victims of a cruel system, press-ganged, starved, flogged and ill-treated to the verge of mutiny. A true portrait lies somewhere between the two. But if it is strictly true, it cannot be more than a sketch.

Most of the sailors were very young men. The average age of the crew of the Victory was 22. Among 703 men on the ship's books, there were only about 40 who were over 40 years of age, but there were 100 who were under 20. Some were 12 or 13, and the youngest, John Doag of Edinburgh, was recorded as 10 years old. They were preponderantly English: 452 Englishmen, 74 Irish, 72 Scots, 24 Welshmen, 28 Americans and 53 assorted foreigners – men from almost every country in Europe, including France, and from India, Africa and the Caribbean. Among them, there was said to have been one woman in disguise.

Probably less than half of them had been forced into the navy by the press-gangs. The rest were either volunteers or 'quota men', who were mostly miscreants sent to the ships as a punishment by magistrates. The proportion pressed into the service had grown as the war against Napoleon progressed, because the navy was expanding, and because it was competing for men with the army, the home defence forces in England, the merchant navy and the privateers. Seamen preferred the merchant navy because the pay was better, and they preferred the privateers because they had more chance of capturing enemy merchant ships and winning prize-money for them.

The press-gangs, which rounded up seamen in the coastal towns and forcibly put them on board the ships of the fleet, were detested in their time and have had an evil reputation ever since. Certainly, they must have caused unhappiness and hardship, because they took their men without a moment's warning. But they were only a primitive form of the conscription that modern citizens suffer in time of war. It was bad luck to be caught by them, but it was only bad luck because other people managed to escape: in those days men escaped by hiding or running fast; now they escape, if they want to, by subtler more devious means. Most men who were pressed resigned themselves to their fate when they were on board, like modern conscripts, and there was not much distinction between them and the volunteers. Both classes united in despising the quota men, who usually knew nothing about the sea and had a reputation for dirt and thievery.

The senior ratings, and the junior officers, lived on the orlop deck, which was the lowest deck of all, either on or below the waterline. Almost all the rest of the crew lived on the lower gun deck. Both these decks were as dank and dark as dungeons. When the gunports were opened for battle or practice, light and air were let in to the gun deck; but, otherwise, only a dim light filtered down through the gratings which gave access to the hold, and everyone lived by the light of candles and lanterns. On these decks the men ate at mess-tables slung from the beams above, and slept in hammocks fourteen inches apart. Here also, and on the other gun decks, they manned the capstan, the pumps, the massive sodden anchor cables, the galley fire which was the only source of warmth, and the guns themselves – all the working parts of the ship except the sails and rigging and the wheel. Many of them had no reason to go to the upper decks or see the daylight, and they probably seldom did so except to visit the heads – the holes on each side of the bowsprit, under the open sky and over the open sea, which were the only sanitary fittings.

About two-thirds of a crew were watchkeepers: some ships kept three watches, but most kept two, so that watchkeepers were four hours on and four hours off. The other third, who were called idlers, worked by day and slept by night: carpenters, gunners, cooks, sailmakers, signalmen, ropemakers, coopers, barbers and tailors, and the servants, stewards and clerks of the officers. Night or day, the decks were never quiet. Men going on watch were roused with customary shouts and curses. Those coming off watch, perhaps wet through with rain and spray, clambered into hammocks almost as wet as themselves, swinging with the roll of the ship among the bodies of men who were trying to sleep. Long before dawn, all hands were turned out by the pipes and shouts and blows of the boatswain's mates, and hammocks and bedding were lashed up and stowed in nets along the bulwarks of the upper decks, where the fresh air could blow through them and where, in case of battle, they could provide some shelter from splinters and musketry.

The total lack of privacy and comfort was not a cruel whim: it was a necessity, because the ships were built to fight, and when they fought the whole of the deck space was needed to work the guns. To clear the decks for action, all the apparatus of living had to be instantly moved – hammocks stowed, and mess-tables hoisted up to the deckbeams – so that each deck was unobstructed from stem to stern. The bulkheads which shut off the captain's and officers' cabins were movable too, and all the furniture of the cabins could be sent down to the hold, stowed in the ship's boats or hoisted in the rigging – or if the call to action was urgent, hove overboard. An efficient ship could always be cleared in six minutes, the gunports opened, powder brought up from the magazines and shot from the lockers, the guns loaded and run out and ready to fire. And in that process any personal property lying around would certainly have gone through the ports and into the sea. Men learned to be tidy, and if they had private possessions, they learned not to value them too highly.

The huge crews, and hence the overcrowding, were also a fighting necessity. The ships could have been sailed with a tenth of the number of men. It was only in battle they really needed the other nine-tenths – to serve the guns, repel boarders or act as boarders themselves, to put out fires, doctor the wounded, plug shotholes in the hull, and still throughout the battle to sail the ship. The depths of boredom in the blockade were not only due to the sameness of every day, of the food, the scene and the company; they were made deeper because most of the men had nothing essential to do, and most of the tasks they were given were only created to stop them doing nothing. Everyone knew it was useless to holystone the decks every day before breakfast. This kind of duty was given the air of a sacred naval custom, but all it did was occupy the hands of a few hundred men at an awkward time of day. Nothing was done to occupy their minds.

Their only lawful pleasure was the rum ration, and their only sustaining hope was for prize-money. In theory, the whole value of a captured ship was distributed to the admiral commanding the station, and the officers and men of the ship that captured it. The proportions were often varied by Acts of Parliament, and the seamen's share was small. Sometimes, a single happy fight could make a captain rich for the rest of his life, and give each of his seamen about enough cash to get drunk on. But still, prize-money was the dream of every man, and indeed it was the basis of most of the navy's tactics.

From this life there was no relief until the ship needed extensive repairs and the crew was paid off: that might be in two years, or it might be in fifteen. Meanwhile, no man normally left the ship unless he was dead or seriously ill. In port, shore leave was seldom granted for fear of desertion; instead of it, cargoes of prostitutes were brought on board. In one frigate which returned to Plymouth from the blockade of Brest with a crew of three hundred and seven, the women on board were counted next morning: there were three hundred and nine. A few captains, it was true, had tried the experiment of letting their men go ashore, and the men had been so touched and surprised at this kindness that they had nearly all come back. One captain proudly claimed that he had lost fewer men that way than a neighbouring ship which had its boats rowing round it all night to watch for swimmers. But this was rare. The Victory, after two years on blockade, and before Trafalgar, was three weeks in Portsmouth harbour: the officers went ashore, but not the crew – probably not even the score of men whose homes were in the town.

And yet, in all these circumstances, something like a miracle was achieved. The fleet was manned by thousands and thousands of ignorant uneducated men. Half of them had no wish to be where they were. Perhaps a sixth were beggars and convicts. They were herded in a confinement worse than prison with nothing constructive to do. And they became the most excellent navy the world had ever seen. Partly this was done by iron-hard discipline. But discipline could not have been enough. There had to be leadership too, and the leadership was brilliant.

It had to start with discipline: nobody could sail a square-rigged ship without it, if only because the ship was operated entirely by human muscle, and one man in a crew who did not pull his weight was a liability and often a danger to the rest. To enforce the discipline, the most fearsome punishments were provided by law and tradition – the hangings from the yardarm, the ceremonial floggings with the cat, running the gauntlet, flogging round the fleet – and the custom of 'starting', by which a boatswain's mate who transmitted an officer's order to the men would follow it instantly by lashing out with a rope's end. Some such punishments had to exist, and these at least were practical; but in Nelson's time, people were beginning to discover that if they were known to exist they seldom had to be used. Officially, the power of captains to inflict them was beginning to be restrained; in the year after Trafalgar, captains were told not to order more than twelve lashes without a court martial. But still, a captain at sea was king of his domain, and did very much as he pleased. There was still endless scope for a sadist, or for a weak man who was basically afraid of the unruly mob of men he had to command. Everything depended on the captain's character. Sometimes a crew took the risk, which was close to mutiny, of protesting against their captain to the commander-in-chief. But sometimes, when a ship was paid off, they subscribed to give the captain a present, and begged to join him on his next appointment. There were happy ships, and ships where life was hell.

The only certain glimpse of what the sailors thought about it all was given by the mutinies at Spithead and the Nore in 1797. The mutineers on that occasion risked their lives by their defiance: the demands they were ready to die for seem now pathetically humble. They did not protest against the punishments, only against the unfair use of them. They asked for more pay, since they were paid less than soldiers; and that men wounded in battle should continue to be paid until they were better; and that pay should not be withheld, as it often was for years. And they asked for shore leave, for vegetables when they could be obtained, and for a fairer share of prize-money. Beyond that, they had nothing to say against the laws and customs of the navy, only against the people who broke them – unjust officers, unscrupulous paymasters and pursers, and doctors who ate or embezzled the special food provided for their patients. They turned some officers out of their ships, but respected those who had treated them fairly according to the rules. It is hard to believe that these sailors accepted every other hardship without protesting, even when they had taken such risks to create an opportunity. But it was so, and one has to remember that theirs was a cruel age, when elegant wealth was founded on brutal poverty. Life afloat was hard, but so was life ashore. Nelson himself, coming back from the sea, was shocked and distressed at the living conditions of farm labourers near his home in Norfolk.

Not only the hardship extended to life afloat: so did the elegance. Not everybody ate maggots – at least, not all the time. Admirals and captains lived in cabins furnished and decorated with the impeccable taste of the age, and maintained the civilized life of eighteenth-century gentlemen. Their cabin doors opened on to the squalor of the gun decks, but nobody worried about the contrast, on either side of the door. Dr. Gillespie, who wrote the letter to his sister, described a day as a member of Nelson's staff on blockade in the Mediterranean. The admiral rose at six, and his officers assembled in his dining cabin for breakfast – tea, hot rolls, toast and cold tongue. From seven until two, all of them worked at the business of the day. From two o'clock, a band of music played on deck, and at 2.45 the admiral's dinner was announced with drums and the tune of 'The Roast Beef of Old England'. Dinner lasted from three until half past four or five: three courses, a dessert of fruit, three or four of the finest wines, coffee and liqueurs. After it, the band played again and the diners walked the deck until six, when tea was announced; and at eight a rummer of punch with cake or biscuits.

Perhaps Gillespie had joined the ship at a lucky moment when she had just been revictualled. There were certainly times when even the admiral's cooks had nothing to work with except the salt beef and biscuit in the hold. But Nelson's dinners were well known among the officers of his fleet; the food and drink were better than their own, and he was a host of unequalled charm. Whenever the weather was fine and the enemy quiescent, the flags which signalled his invitations were hoisted and eagerly acknowledged by his guests. He did not care very much what he ate or drank, and he was often on a self-imposed diet: but he liked to give pleasure, and his hospitality was part of his technique for keeping a fleet contented and efficient. Captains led lonely lives, and after an invitation to his flagship they were rowed back to their own ships revived by an afternoon of good living and conversation and spellbound afresh by his friendship. It was important, for these were the men on whom the miracle depended.

The captains, good or bad, were certainly different from their crews. They were almost a generation older than the average, men on either side of forty. All of them had been in the navy since they were eleven or twelve, when their parents sent them to sea as the nominal servants of a captain who was a relative or a friend. Most of them were happily married: they seldom saw their wives or children, but they were prolific writers of letters. And the most important difference was that they were gentry.

This social distinction, despised by most modern people, was the backbone of Nelson's navy, as it was of Wellington's army. Clever men of the lower classes could rise through the ranks of warrant officers to become boatswains, masters-at-arms and ultimately ships' masters. But they hardly ever crossed to the other superior ladder, by which boys climbed to be midshipmen, lieutenants, captains and admirals. To start on that ladder a boy needed parents who knew a naval captain, or somehow could earn a captain's patronage. So naval officers were a clique, even more compact and exclusive than the army officers' clique. They were not aristocrats – those went into the army: by and large, they were country squires, and preponderantly squires from the southern counties of England. Nelson, coming from Norfolk, was unusual, and Collingwood, who came from Northumberland, was always an outsider. The few, very few, who had risen from lower walks of life were often despised by their crews for

their humble origin. The crew of one frigate protested against
their captain's cruelty: and one of their complaints was that he
was the son of a barber. Men felt they had a right to be
commanded by gentlemen.

It was a system that made no pretence of fairness. But fairness
was not what mattered: what mattered was that the squires of
southern England were proud of the navy. They had always
been so since the time of Elizabeth, and for hundreds of years
before that, they had been equally proud to be pirates.

That deep-rooted pride must have been the first cause of the
astonishing efflorescence of naval power and skill that they
brought about. Before the war against France, the navy had
had its evil days, when its reputation was low. But for years
before Trafalgar, it alone had been in contact with the enemy,
while the army was land-bound at home. It had won some
famous victories, and it could be seen to be the country's first
defence; so it had risen high in the esteem of English people. In
the bad times, the pride had been latent: with praise and success
it grew, and the captains who felt it instilled it in the hetero-
geneous men they had to command.

They would not have succeeded if they had not also, in the
same few years, had a change of heart. Perhaps the mutiny of
1797 did some good. It did not win the sailors all they asked for,
but it did show that they had a corporate opinion. Whether that
was the partial cause or not, the captains who were at sea in 1805
were a different stamp of men from the thoughtless autocrats
who caused the mutiny. They were still autocrats, but on the
whole they were thoughtful for their people. None of the active
admirals would have tolerated the tyranny of the generation
before them. They had tyrants' powers and most of them used
them wisely, and so they were doubly strong.

Nobody can say how much of this revolution could have
been caused by a single man's example. But it was a fact that
the most successful admiral, the national hero of three of the
victories, was a man who was vain, irascible, unfaithful to his
wife, brave, kind, compassionate and irresistibly lovable, and

that wherever he flew his flag, pride suddenly flamed in every man in the fleet.

The largest squadrons of Napoleon's fleet were in Toulon and Brest. Perhaps the blockade of Brest, commanded by Cornwallis, was the harder of the two. The northern part of the Bay of Biscay is a notorious stretch of sea, foggy, cold and stormy, where strong tides set through the rocks of the Isle of Ushant. 'Mariners must exercise the greatest caution,' the modern Admiralty Pilot says of it, still with the studied elegance of eighteenth-century style. 'This island is surrounded by dangers; rocks are numerous and some lie far from the land; fogs and thick weather are not uncommon; the tidal streams are strong, and the extent of their influence seaward undetermined . . . Sailing vessels, except those bound from western French ports should not, as a rule, pass in sight of Ouessant (Ushant) but, even with a fair wind, should make good westing, bearing in mind that the prevailing winds and currents have a tendency to set towards Ouessant and into the Bay of Biscay when southward of that island. To get well westward is therefore of the greatest importance.'

No such option existed for the blockading fleet. To keep the approaches to Brest under observation, they had to stay in sight of this lethal shore, or at least to keep their frigates in sight of it; and in the prevailing south-westerly winds, it lay to leeward. By modern standards their ships were unhandy, slow to go about and slow to windward; and probably no modern mariner would dare to explain exactly how they were able to stand off and on, estimating the tidal streams and currents, night and day, summer and winter, constantly solving the problems of navigation and ship-handling – and this not merely in one ship, but in a whole fleet of them. The achievement astonished the French, who looked out every morning and saw the sails still there, and it is still as astonishing now. So is their toughness: anyone, seaman or not, can imagine this life in ships with no shelter on deck and no warmth below, exposed to the rain and fog and to seas with a fetch of several thousand miles. They only relaxed in settled westerly gales when the French could not conceivably have left the harbour: then they ran for shelter in Plymouth Sound, a hundred and fifty miles across the Channel.

In this one respect, Cornwallis's fleet off Brest had the advantage over Nelson's off Toulon: their weather was worse, but they had a home port within reach. They never put in there unless they were forced to, and when they did they were seldom allowed ashore; but at least they could land their sick and ask for dockyard repairs, and perhaps hear some news of their families and the world. Nelson's fleet had no such luck. Their nearest ports under British control were Malta and Gibraltar, each between six and seven hundred miles away – much too far to be any use as bases. So they had to depend entirely on themselves: cure their own sick, repair their own ships, and find their own provisions where they could.

Nelson's policy off Toulon differed from Cornwallis's off Brest. Brest was at the mouth of the English Channel: there, the blockade was intended to keep the French in harbour, and it did. But Nelson's intention, indeed his burning wish, was to lure them out and beat them. So he kept out of sight of Toulon. His frigates watched it, and sometimes he sent a squadron, deliberately weak and tempting, to trail their coats across the harbour mouth. With the bulk of the fleet, he ranged round the seas which were bordered by the coasts of France and Spain in the north and west, Majorca and Minorca in the south, and Sardinia and Corsica in the east. After Spain joined France in 1804, all these shores were hostile except Sardinia, which was primitive but nominally neutral. There, at the northern end of the island, inside the small islands called Maddalena, he found a sheltered anchorage where his ships could get water and wood for the galley fires, and take on board provisions from supply ships which came up from Gibraltar and the towns on the African coast. This anchorage was the only port that his crews had the pleasure of seeing, and its peasants and fishermen were the only people.

In these conditions Nelson took infinite pains to keep his crews healthy and as happy as they could be. He varied the cruising simply to give them another shore to look at, and he varied each day by different kinds of training. Much of his thought and correspondence was spent in the search for food, which often had to be bought clandestinely from people who were afraid of Napoleon. His emissaries bought cattle in Africa, and huge quantities of lemon juice in Italy and Sicily, and they were always looking for onions, which the conservative sailors liked and he believed were exceptionally good for them. In Maddalena, they fished for tuna, and managed to buy some fruit. For two years, through his exertions, they lived off the country: men died of the ills they would have died of anywhere, especially consumption; but at the end of it all the survivors were as healthy as when they started. After twenty months off Toulon, there was only one man sick in the Victory. It was an achievement in seamanship equal to the struggle against the weather off Brest, for normally, in the navy, at least ten times as many men were killed by accident and disease as were ever killed in battle. His own health suffered more than most. He always worried about it, perhaps unduly, and he was always seasick in bad weather; but now, he knew he was slowly going blind.

And through the incessant sailing and practice at sea, the mob of men he started with became perfectly trained: every man and boy had his action station and knew precisely what he had to do. They longed to do it. As month after month went by, off the port which they aptly called Too-Long, they came more and more to despise the French who would not come out and fight; for a final fight was the only end they could see to the changeless bondage of the life they led, and they knew they would win it. Meanwhile, they dreamed about home, but were quite out of touch with the land they were there to defend.

But to put Trafalgar finally in perspective, one has to glance at the England they dreamed about. One aspect of it seems familiar now to any Englishman old enough to remember 1940.

Napoleon threatened invasion and so did Hitler, and the threats united the English as nothing else could. The nation armed its defenders on both occasions with absurdly obsolete weapons, including pikes – perhaps the same pikes; and on both occasions the people as a whole were determined, or said they were, to repel the invaders with pitchforks and kitchen knives, or anything else that came to hand. They alarmed each other with rumours of secret weapons, and encouraged each other with stories that the invasion had already been tried and had failed. Men dressed up in unfamiliar uniforms, which made some of them feel brave and some ridiculous. They drilled on village greens, and laughed at each other's clumsiness or their own; and they earnestly manned the same stretches of the coast, and patrolled the seas offshore in fishing boats which had hastily been armed.

Even the means of invasion were much the same, and the same phrase was in use to describe them: flat-bottomed boats. Napoleon and Hitler both assembled fleets of boats in the ports on the other side of the Straits of Dover, and armies which were ready to embark. But neither army did embark – and for comparable reasons. To cross the Channel, Hitler needed command of the air, and he fought for it and lost it in the Battle of Britain. Napoleon needed command of the sea, and he finally lost it in the Battle of Trafalgar. And both tyrants, abandoning their plans, turned their armies to new adventures in eastern Europe.

But one difference between these threats to England was their length. Hitler's only lasted for a single hectic summer, but Napoleon's lasted from 1797 to 1805, with only the brief uncertain pause at the time of the Peace of Amiens in 1801. Almost a whole generation of children went to bed every night with the fear of Frenchmen lurking in the dark. By 1805, people were tired of living in alarm. The humour of it had begun to wear thin: not even the professional cartoonists could think of jokes about Bonaparte that were new. The determination was still there, but defence was well organized and so was no longer amusing. By then, responsible people believed invasion could be defeated, but that sober belief was less inspiring to the English temperament than sharpening carving knives.

When Napoleon had to abandon his plan, he said he had never meant to do it anyway, it had only been a feint. This was the kind of prop to their self-esteem that only small children or dictators use with any hope of being believed. Some of his most devoted followers did believe it, but they had not seen his correspondence, as historians have. In fact, the threat was real: of all his conquests, this was the one he most passionately wanted – not only to humiliate England, but also to open the seas to further world-wide conquests. In the summer of 1805, he spent much of his time at Boulogne, inspecting the troops assembled there and the thousands of boats, and contemplating the twenty miles of sea to the cliffs of Dover, and waiting, with growing impatience, for his fleet to come up the Channel. On August 22nd he wrote to one of his admirals: 'I trust you have arrived in Brest. Do not lose a moment. Come into the Channel, bring our united fleet, and England is ours. We are all ready; everything is embarked. If you are only here for twenty-four hours, all will be over, and six centuries of shame and insult will be avenged.'

This was the one essential. In the absence of his fleet, there was no doubt who commanded the Straits of Dover. English frigates were always on patrol, a few hundred yards outside the range of the batteries of Boulogne, and the smaller harbours of Etaples, Ambleteuse and Wimereux. The French boats could only move from port to port because there are shoals along that shore, and they were too shallow for the frigates. But fleets of English boats could cross the Channel with impunity, and sometimes did so, armed with small guns or with torpedoes – floating fused explosive charges, which drifted into the harbours with the tide – or with the rockets recently invented by William Congreve, which the First Lord of the Admiralty mistrusted, and described disdainfully as a 'romantic form of warfare'. These attacks sometimes sank a few boats or set them on fire, but they cost many lives and did no decisive damage to the mass of boats which were crammed inside the harbours. The threat remained.

It was strange that among all the rumours of secret weapons, nobody on either side seemed to give a thought to the one invention that could have upset the balance in the Straits: steam. People in England believed Napoleon was digging a Channel tunnel, and possessed troop-carrying balloons or monstrous rafts, which were fitted with forts and carried ten thousand men, and were propelled by a paddle-wheel at each corner, rotated by a windmill. Yet among these nightmares, nobody dreamed of the little steamboat Charlotte Dundas, which since 1801 had been peacefully pulling barges along the Forth and Clyde Canal in Scotland: nor, in France, did they think of the steamer that Robert Fulton, the American engineer, had built in Paris in 1803. A very few steam tugboats, on a calm and misty night when the English warships could not move at all, would instantly have solved Napoleon's problem, without the intervention of his fleet. If he had given the order, they could have been built. Within four years of Trafalgar an open sea passage was made by a steamboat in America, from Hoboken to Philadelphia; and the moment Napoleon's reign was ended, steamers were built in England not merely to cross the narrowest part of the Channel, but to run a passenger service from Brighton to Le Havre. This was the nearest escape that England had, but it seems that the English were not aware of it. Nor did anyone at Trafalgar, so far as one knows, reflect as they slowly sailed into battle that their ships and their art were almost out of date, or that such a sight would never be seen again.

In the winter of 1804 the invasion plan was in abeyance, but on March 2nd, 1805, the Emperor issued new orders to his admirals. Admiral Ganteaume, who commanded the squadron at Brest, of twenty-one ships-of-the-line and six frigates, was ordered to escape, to attack and seize the English flotilla off Ferrol and liberate four French and some Spanish ships that were blockaded there, and then to sail to Martinique in the West Indies.

Admiral Villeneuve, who commanded eleven ships-of-the-line and six frigates in Toulon, was to escape from Nelson and liberate one French ship and whatever Spaniards were ready in Cadiz. Then he was to sail for Martinique and wait there forty days for Admiral Ganteaume. If Ganteaume had not arrived by then, he was to cruise off the Canary Islands to intercept English convoys from India, and then return to Cadiz.

Admiral Missiessy, who had commanded in Rochefort, had already escaped with a small force, and he was also told to join the others in Martinique. A further half-dozen ships were waiting on the West Indian station.

So an enormous fleet, of forty French ships, perhaps twenty or thirty Spaniards and at least a dozen frigates, would be secretly assembled. It was then to return to Ushant, take the English by surprise and sail up Channel.

On March 30th, following this order, Villeneuve and his squadron left Toulon, and the long blockade began to break up in the war of movement which finally brought the fleets together six and a half months later off Cadiz.

The basis of this grandiose plan, the meeting in the West Indies, was known in England quickly. There is a romantic half-forgotten story of a spy in Paris, known only as l'Ami, who reported it, on the very day the Emperor's order was issued, to the Russian Ambassador in Dresden. The Ambassador kept the news to himself until May, but in April another spy sent it straight to London, and added the fascinating detail that the admiral at Brest had nine hundred thousand francs in his coffers. But the news could not be quickly sent to Nelson off Toulon. In his anxiety to lure the French out, he had set his net too loosely: two of his frigates followed the French fleet, sailing south, but then left it to report to him in Sardinia. All these months he had had to make his own guesses of Napoleon's strategy, and he guessed wrong: he watched for the French in the east. It was not until May 10th, after a month of the most intense worry of his career, that he heard for certain from an Englishman in Portugal that they were bound for the Indies. By then, it was common knowledge in England, or at least a common assumption: the *Morning Chronicle* had reported it the day before, and added that nobody in England could sleep in peace at night.

The moves of that anxious summer can quickly be summarized. The Emperor's original plan broke down at once, because Ganteaume could not escape from Brest. When he received his orders, he could see fifteen English sail outside the harbour, and he offered to go out and fight them. But Napoleon replied that a battle then and there would be useless: he must escape unseen. That was impossible. He tried but was seen at once, and so he put back into harbour, and there he stayed.*

Meanwhile Napoleon had been to Italy, where he was wrongly informed that Nelson was looking for Villeneuve in Egypt. That gave him new ideas. Villeneuve, he concluded, was in the West Indies and free from interference: why should he not use his time in capturing British possessions there? He sent a series of new and different orders by frigates and other ships across to Martinique. They arrived in the wrong order, and in some respects they contradicted each other; but the essence of them, put together, was that Villeneuve was to spend a month in capturing all the British colonies he could, and was then to return to Europe. He was to pick up fifteen Spanish ships that were said to be ready in Ferrol, and sail to Brest. There he would defeat the blockading squadron and free Ganteaume to join him in the Channel.

This was a madly ambitious scheme that only revealed the Emperor's ignorance of naval limitations. The original plan had had an element of surprise, but this had none. It expected a

* The outermost bay of the harbour of Brest is called Bertheaume, and a Frenchman of the time drafted an epitaph which may be translated:

Here lies the Admiral Ganteaume,
Who, when the wind was in the east,
Sailed out from Brest towards Bertheaume;
And, when the wind was in the west,
Turned round, and sailed back to Brest.

major battle off Brest, against an English fleet that would be forewarned of it. The battle would have to be fought before Ganteaume could join it. Villeneuve was expected to fight it with his own fleet, after a double crossing of the Atlantic and a month of fighting in the Indies, and with the addition of a Spanish fleet whose ships and admiral he could not even name. Confused by the contradictions and desolated by such an impossible task, Villeneuve began faithfully to try to perform it. He attacked a small British island. But then he had news that the Emperor's premise was wrong: Nelson, far from being in Egypt, had followed him across the Atlantic and now was close behind him.

In this dilemma Villeneuve deserved more sympathy than he has usually received. Was he to carry on with the Emperor's plan of capturing islands? If he had, he would certainly have had to fight Nelson, and could not expect after that to be fit for the second and more important part of the operations. He decided to sail for Europe as soon as he could. History blamed him for not waiting for Ganteaume, and for being afraid of Nelson, and so did many men in his fleet who did not know his orders. But in fact, he knew that Ganteaume was not coming, and whether he was afraid of Nelson or not, he was right to avoid a battle in the Caribbean.

His voyage back was slow, against contrary winds. The English knew he was coming, and off Cape Finisterre on July 22nd a squadron under Sir Robert Calder intercepted him and an inconclusive battle was fought in a fog. His ships were in bad repair and thousands of his men were sick: in stormy weather, alternating with calms, he made for the nearest port, which was not Ferrol but Vigo.

Nelson came back behind him with his fleet in much better shape and put in to Gibraltar; with no news, he then sailed north to join the Channel fleet off Brest. Villeneuve went up to Ferrol, as he had been ordered, and put to sea again on August 13th. By then he knew the most powerful fleet the English could assemble must be waiting for him in the Channel mouth, and he knew his own fleet was no match for it. The situation, he thought, had changed entirely since the Emperor's orders were written so many months before. In the dark one night he saw the lights of another fleet and concluded it was English. He was wrong, it was French; but that, with contrary winds, decided his mind. He turned south to Cadiz – the option given to him in the Emperor's first order.

Off Cadiz, Admiral Collingwood was waiting with a small blockading squadron. It kept out of the way to let Villeneuve go in; and slowly, over the next six weeks, the English fleets assembled to keep him there.

OFF SHORE

Cuthbert Collingwood was a strange kind of man to be an admiral. He was conscientious, capable, shrewd and unquestionably brave: as a strategist he always seemed to know better than anyone else what the French intended to do. But he was also scholarly, pedantic, puritan and dour – at the age of 55, a fatherly or even grandfatherly figure in the fleet. He made a good admiral, but he might have made a better bishop.

Like most of the other officers, he had been in the navy since he was 11, and nobody in either fleet can have been so long at sea. Of those forty-four years, he had only spent six on shore; and after Trafalgar he stayed at sea until he died, still at sea, in 1810. It was not that he wanted to: on the contrary, he was married and had two daughters and always longed to go home and become a normal family man. Only an overpowering sense of duty kept him sailing. His hobby, a little pathetic in such a life, was gardening. He especially liked to plant groves of oaks on his modest estate in Northumberland. 'If the country gentlemen do not make it a point to plant oaks,' he wrote when he was at sea blockading Brest, 'the time will not be very distant when, to keep our Navy, we must depend entirely on captures from the enemy . . . I wish every body thought on this subject as I do; they would not walk through their farms without a pocketful of acorns to drop in the hedge-sides, and then let them take their chance.' The wooden navy seemed eternal.

He had a reputation for being stern and strict, and yet of being just, and he seems to have been well respected on the lower deck. A boy named Robert Hay, who served under him in

the Channel fleet in 1804, went so far as to say that a better
seaman, or a better friend to seamen, never trod a quarter-deck.
But he never unbent with his men, and not often with anyone
else. Aboard his ship he mainly enjoyed the company of his dog:
its name was Bounce, and it slept by his cot and had reconciled
itself to a life at sea, except that it hated guns.

But in spite of his idiosyncrasies, Collingwood set an example
of the change that was coming over the navy. Years before, as a
young captain, he had always kept a log of the punishments he
ordered, and part of it still exists. In four months he ordered a
dozen men from six to a dozen lashes. Four were for drunken-
ness and fighting, two were for theft, three for absence from duty
or sleeping as a sentinel; one man had broken rules by bringing
liquor on board, and one had spread malicious reports of a
sergeant of marines. The last received seven lashes 'for beating
Stephen Shore, a poor silly boy'. Clearly these were offences that
had to be punished somehow. But later in his career he
remarked, it was said: 'I cannot for the life of me comprehend
the religion of an officer who could pray all one day and flog his
men all the next.' And accordingly he gave up corporal punishment, and succeeded in keeping the strictest of discipline by
watering offenders' grog or giving them extra ignominious duties
– and sometimes by moral lectures which were dreaded by his
younger officers. Robert Hay remembered that a look of dis-
pleasure from him was worse than a dozen lashes. When he was
out of earshot, young midshipmen sometimes laughed at him,
but always half in awe and half in affection: one of them, who
wrote about him when he was old himself, remembered that
they called him old Cuddy.

This curious man was nine years older than Nelson, and could
hardly have been less like him. But Nelson's friendship em-
braced all kinds of people, and the two of them had been friends
for nearly thirty years, since they were lieutenants in the West
Indies – where among other things they had drawn well-known
but not very skilful portraits of each other. 'My dear Coll,'
Nelson still began the letters he often wrote him; or sometimes

'My dearest Friend.' And Collingwood replied as warmly, with only the touch of respect that Nelson's quicker promotion had come to demand: 'I am, my dear friend, affectionately yours.'

Collingwood had spent the past two years, or most of them, among the tides and rocks of Ushant, which he said had more danger in them than a battle once a week. It had left him in low spirits, and tired to death of it all. But he also knew only too well the view of Cadiz from the sea: he had blockaded the place for years, before the Peace of Amiens, back in the 1790s. And he had lain there another three months, all that summer of 1805, when on August 20th he saw the enemy fleet bearing down on him from Cape St. Vincent. He took it lightly. 'I must tell you,' he wrote to his wife, 'what a squeeze we had like to have got yesterday. While we were cruising off the town, down came the combined fleet of thirty-six sail of men-of-war: we were only three poor things, with a frigate and a bomb, and drew off towards the Straits, not very ambitious, as you may suppose, to try our strength against such odds . . . I hope I shall have somebody come to me soon, and in the mean time I must take the best care of myself I can. This is a comfortless station, on which it is difficult to procure refreshment, except the grapes which the Portuguese bring us . . . Pray tell me all you can think about our family, and about the beauties of your domain – the oaks, the woodlands, and the verdant meads.'

He sent the news to England, and his letter with it, by the fast frigate Euryalus, Captain Blackwood – a ship and a captain who were to play a leading part in the drama that was beginning. And he settled down with his puny squadron off the harbour mouth, frequently sending signals to an imaginary fleet at sea – an old trick which was not very likely to deceive the enemy but might, he hoped, sow a little doubt in their minds.

Reinforcements soon began to come in – sightings of distant sails at dawn, suspense until flags could be seen, then recognition signals and perhaps a shout or a cheer; on August 22nd, four ships that had been blockading Cartagena, and on the 28th the whole of Sir Robert Calder's fleet of eighteen sail – twenty-two more ships, each with a character and reputation of its own. There, for example, was the Prince, which was said to sail like a haystack, and the Spartiate, which sailed like a witch and must have been built of stolen timber, seamen said, because she sailed better at night than she did in the day. With Calder were seven of Nelson's Mediterranean fleet which had sailed with him to the Indies and back again, among them the Conqueror, Leviathan and Swiftsure, painted proudly in his personal style, black hulls, black gunports and two bands of yellow, so that when the ports were closed the ships looked chequered. From Cartagena came the Minotaur and Bellerophon, which had fought at the Battle of the Nile, and the Tonnant, a superb French ship admired by every connoisseur, which had been captured there.*

And with twenty-two more ships, there were twenty-two more captains for Collingwood to command, all men of strong personality, and each with idiosyncrasies of his own. There, for one, was Captain Thomas Fremantle of the Neptune: flamboyant, quick-tempered, intolerant, a man with a gallant eye for a pretty girl, a ponderous sense of humour, and an appetite for wine, which gave him bile. He was a climber: he had acquired the powerful Lord Buckingham as a patron and an heiress named Betsey as a wife. To him, he wrote sycophantically; and to her, loving bombastic heavy-handed letters in which he playfully called her Tussy, or Mrs. Tussy, or sometimes Little Woman. They had three children, and she was expecting a fourth at any moment – 'I desire if it is a boy you will have him

---

* This was the second British ship to arrive with a French name: Collingwood already had the Achille. So perhaps this is the moment to mention that ships which were captured, and so changed sides, usually kept their names. On the other hand, having lost a ship, whatever the reason, both navies often gave the same name to a new one. So at Trafalgar, the British had the Tonnant, Temeraire and Belleisle and the small cutter Entreprenante; the French had the *Berwick*; both sides had an Achille and a Swiftsure. Also there was a British Neptune, a French *Neptune* and a Spanish *Neptuno*. In the hope of avoiding confusion, the names of ships in the British fleet are printed in this book in Roman type, and the names of ships in the French and Spanish fleet are in italics.

christened Stephen, and if it is a girl that you will name it Louisa,
I can't bear your popery names.' Evidently, theirs was a family
home where father's word was law, and when she wrote to tell
him of small decisions she had made, about the management of
the estate, or the servants, or the carriages, he complimented the
little woman on her cleverness. Some wives would have been
infuriated by his condescending air, but to do him justice she
seemed to like his treatment.

Fremantle was certainly not a man to suffer a pedantic
scholarly admiral with any patience at all. But he did not meet
him, and perhaps it was just as well. Collingwood was absorbed
in the details of administration, and the importance of keeping
watch on the French, and he had no time for sociable frivolity.
To the surprise of the captains who joined him, none of them
were invited to the flagship; and, which was worse, he discouraged them from visiting each other. The weather was fine
and calm, boats could easily be launched, and all of them
wanted to call on their friends for some gossip, a drink and
dinner – or, more seriously, to discuss their future tactics. But
there they were, with old friends sometimes in hailing distance,
yet each shut up in his own ship with his own subordinates,
whose faces and conversation he already knew too well. They
felt resentful. Brest and Toulon had been boring enough, but
this was more frustrating. Fremantle confessed to Betsey that he
had nothing to do and his temper was getting worse. So was his
bile. He tried to cure it, and to pass the time, by brewing spruce
beer in his cabin and drinking less wine. His first lieutenant, he
told her, had been in the ship much longer than he had and
could not bear the smallest contradiction, his steward was a
drunkard, his servant was insolent, and the only goat on board
had fallen down a hatchway during a storm off Brest, so he had
to drink tea without milk for his breakfast. It was a life of misery,
he said.

Probably every captain would have agreed. 'We have got into
the clutches of another stay-on-board Admiral'; so Captain
Codrington of the Orion wrote, although he was not at all a

man of Fremantle's sort. He was younger, only 35, and he had a philosophical serious turn of mind: he looked for the best in people while Fremantle looked for the worst. Orion was his first appointment to command a line-of-battle ship, and it was only three weeks since he had sailed her out of Plymouth. He had been married for two years to a girl called Jane, whom other people besides himself described as a beauty, and this was the first time he had left her, and his year-old son and new-born baby. The pain of the parting had not worn off yet, and when he was alone he was very homesick. 'On the quarter-deck I am the captain,' he wrote to her; 'in my cabin I am the husband and the father.' And Collingwood's ruling left him often in his cabin, and alone.

He was also worried about Sir Robert Calder. Admiral Calder was junior to Collingwood, and so had become second in command. But he was depressed in his spirits, and had asked to go home and said he was too worn to serve any longer; for news had come of a public outcry against him in England for not having followed up the battle of July 22nd, and for letting the French escape. He felt this was injustice: he had been out-numbered, but had attacked and had captured two Spanish ships. All the captains agreed with him: criticism by landsmen and politicians always united the navy. Calder had always been a hospitable man, and had many friends in the fleet. All of them wanted to visit him and give him the sympathy he needed: Codrington, for one, thought it cruel that he should be left alone when he was in such distress. The only chance they had to show him their feelings came three weeks after they had reached Cadiz, when a court martial brought twenty of them together on his ship. After the business was over, they made it a gay occasion – Calder entertained them with dinner, wine and the music of his ship's band – but the gaiety only made them wish it could happen more often, and they privately grumbled together at Collingwood's puritan conscience. 'Content alone is happiness,' Codrington wrote to his wife in one of his philosophical moods. There was very little content in the fleet, he believed – and he was thinking not only of the officers but of the lower deck as well.

And Collingwood, worrying over all the minutest details of the organization of the fleet, was writing home too: Bounce was his only company, he said, and he was indeed a good fellow. 'I am fully determined, if I can get home and manage it properly, to go on shore next spring for the rest of my life; for I am very weary. There is no end to my business; I am at work from morning till even . . . What I look to as the first and great object, is to defeat the projects of this [French and Spanish] fleet, of whom I can get little information; but I watch them narrowly, and if they come out will fight them merrily.' And undoubtedly he would have done so. But he had not told his captains how he meant to do it.

For a month the ships lay there, almost still in the warm autumnal sun, and the boredom and discontent hung over them like a fog. 'For charity's sake, send us Lord Nelson, oh ye men of power!' So Codrington exclaimed, in the privacy of a letter to his wife.

Nelson was at Merton, south-west of London, in the house he had bought for himself and Sir William and Lady Hamilton; for after the chase to the Indies, the Victory had been ordered home to Portsmouth.

Nelson was a man of two loves: his compassionate love for the men with whom he spent his working life, and his passionate love for Lady Hamilton. In a study of Trafalgar, one is mainly concerned with the first of these, and the unique effect it had on his fellow men; but one cannot neglect the woman he thought and spoke about when he was dying.

Emma Hamilton has often been harshly judged. But of course the judgements of history often reflect the moral standards of the historian's era, not of the subject's. Emma had many misfortunes in her life, and another after her death: the misfortune that a series of biographers of Nelson wrote about her in Victorian times. Nowadays, few people could have the heart to condemn her as freely as they did. She was born in poverty, illiterate, outstandingly beautiful in her early teens, without a father and with a mother who was not averse to living off her daughter's earnings; so she was a natural victim of an age when rich men bought and sold their mistresses. And she was a victim too of her own capacity for love, for she fell in love with one of her early protectors, Charles Greville, and was heart-broken when, to pay off his debts, he sold her at the age of 21 to his uncle who was 56.

This was Sir William Hamilton, the British envoy at the court of Naples, an amateur archaeologist, an expert on volcanoes, and a notable collector of works of art. He played Pygmalion. She was an apt and eager girl, and his education succeeded, better perhaps than he hoped. She became the confidante of the Queen of Naples, and when Hamilton was persuaded to marry her, after living with her for seven years, it was largely for her political usefulness: he remarked at the time that he would be superannuated while she was still a young woman.

In 1798, when Nelson arrived in Naples triumphant and wounded from the Battle of the Nile, Hamilton was 67, Emma was 32 and Nelson himself was 40: Nelson already a national hero, Emma still beautiful and influential at the court, and Hamilton ageing quickly and longing for scholarly peace, not for political upheavals or the attentions of an emotional wife.

It used to be said of Emma that she seduced Nelson for the sake of reflected glory. That was uncharitable. Nobody can know how much she loved him: most of her letters to him were destroyed, but most of his to her were carefully preserved. It should be sufficient to know that she had qualities – skill as a lover, shrewdness and common sense, a sailorly sense of humour and a capacity for giving admiration – which made him devoted to her until he died.

His naval friends were always afraid he was making a fool of himself over Emma, and that she would distract him from duty and from his own high standards of behaviour. In the early days she did. His love for her also forced him inevitably into the only notable unkindness of his life, his rejection of Lady Nelson. He had married her when he was 29, in the West Indies where Englishwomen were rare. His letters to her, before and after the wedding, spoke of respect, not love – totally different from the adoring letters he wrote to Emma; and she was undoubtedly a respectable woman – respectable and pathetically dull. To have returned to her unalluring domesticity after Emma might well have broken Nelson's spirit at the height of his career.

Nelson was guilty of that unkindness; but it is absurd to believe him guilty also of deceiving Hamilton. Hamilton was a man of the world who perfectly understood the problem he had foreseen so long before: himself growing old and his wife remaining irrepressible, sociable, gay and ambitious. He was still fond of her, although he sometimes found her exasperating, and he was very fond of Nelson, as all men were. Something had to be done to keep Emma happy: nothing could have been better than for her to fall in love with the man he most admired. He exchanged Emma's tempestuous lovemaking for Nelson's companionship. All three agreed that the house at Merton should belong in the end to the one that lived longest, and they lived together there in amity. Hamilton and Emma had had no child, nor had Nelson and his wife, but in 1801 a daughter was born: to observe the proprieties, she was sent to live with a nurse and always referred to in correspondence as Horatia Nelson Thompson. Both the lovers were with Hamilton when he died, and in his will he bequeathed his favourite portrait of Emma to Nelson, 'my dearest friend, the most virtuous, loyal and truly brave character I ever met with. God bless him, and shame fall on those who do not say amen.'

That was only a month before Nelson left England to begin the blockade of Toulon, and when he came back, two years and a quarter later, whatever scandalous stories had been told were old and almost forgotten. He was only at Merton, on this final visit, a little over three weeks, and he expected at every moment of them to be called back to sea again. But those weeks were a foretaste of the happy home life he had dreamed of at sea. Emma and Horatia were there, and a crowd of his own

relations, and visitors constantly came and went; while in
London, wherever he was seen, crowds gathered to cheer him.
He loved it all. People have searched his letters and reports of his
conversations to find the slightest sign that Emma had any less
enchantment, but there is none. He did not want to go back to
sea. Only one thing could have dragged him away again: if his
friends in the fleet were to fight the French at last, he wanted to
lead them.

Captain Blackwood, whom Collingwood had sent with the
news that the French were in Cadiz, reached Portsmouth on
September 2nd and called at Merton at five o'clock in the
morning on his way to London. Nelson was up and dressed. 'I
am sure you bring me news of the French and Spanish fleets,' he
said at once, 'and I think I shall yet have to beat them.' After ten
more busy days he went to rejoin the Victory, and on the road to
Portsmouth he made a famous entry in his diary: 'At half past
ten drove from dear dear Merton, where I left all which I hold
dear in this world . . .' At Portsmouth, he tried to avoid the
crowds by embarking at an unusual part of the shore, but they
followed him, and people knelt down and blessed him as he
passed.

On September 28th the fleet off Cadiz sighted the Victory to the
westward, wearing his flag. 'Lord Nelson is arrived,' Codrington
wrote to his wife. 'A sort of general joy has been the con-
sequence.'

A great many people have tried to explain the unique respon-
se that Nelson could win from almost everyone. All such
explanations must be more or less subjective: in such a many-
sided character, everyone can choose the aspects that might
have attracted him. And everyone so inclined can find something to disapprove of. Some people in retrospect dislike what
they read of his boyish vanity, or what seems his self-pity when
he was feeling ill. Some, of course, disapprove of his love for
Emma, and some in the nineteenth century were so embarrassed
by his dying exclamation 'Kiss me, Hardy' – although it was

perfectly in character – that they invented the theory that what he said was 'Kismet'. Now, we are perhaps a little nearer than the intervening generations to the moral values of Georgian England: we value kindliness more than strict rectitude, and we can be glad he was not a saint and like him better for it. At any rate, nobody can understand Trafalgar without honestly trying to understand why Nelson was loved so dearly by his fellow men, even though this may only mean adding one more subjective view to those that are past.

The fleet off Cadiz was new. It had never sailed before as a single fleet, and only six of its captains had been under Nelson's command. But that is not to say that the captains were strangers to each other, or to him. There were not very many captains senior enough to command a ship-of-the-line, and all of them had been officers all their lives: the chances are that all of them had met before, somewhere, in years of voyaging. Codrington had not met Nelson, but he was young and new to command, and must have been an exception; and of course every one of them, and every man in the fleet, knew Nelson by reputation. But even if there had been a man in the fleet who had never heard of him, he would very soon have learned, because Nelson in those last three weeks of his life showed all the qualities the reputation had grown on – the bravery, clear thinking, under-standing and tact, and the sudden unpremeditated kindness.

Codrington learned at once. Nelson called him on board the Victory, greeted him in a friendly informal manner, and gave him a letter from his wife: being entrusted with it by a lady, he said, he made a point of delivering it himself. Fremantle was summoned too. 'Would you like a boy or a girl?' the commander-in-chief inquired. Fremantle said a girl. 'Then be content,' Nelson said, and told him that Betsey had had one and was well. And Captain Tyler of the Tonnant: he went to Nelson as soon as he arrived, with a private problem. His son, a young officer, had left his ship in Malta and run away with an opera dancer to Naples, and might be in prison for debt – would Nelson use his influence to save him? Nelson not only wrote to

Naples, but also, without telling Tyler, offered to pay the cost of having the boy set free.

On the day after Victory joined the fleet, Nelson asked half the captains to dine with him, and the day after that, the other half. 'What our late chief will think of this I don't know,' Codrington wrote with glee, 'but I well know what the fleet think of the difference.' The first of those days was Nelson's birthday – he was 47 – and it became a birthday party, combined with what would now be called a briefing. His guests made it plain how glad they were to see him. Their reception, he wrote, was the sweetest sensation of his life. 'The officers who came on board to welcome my return, forgot my rank as commander-in-chief in the enthusiasm with which they greeted me.' And he vividly described the briefing to Lady Hamilton: 'When I came to explain to them the "Nelson touch", it was like an electric shock. Some shed tears, all approved – "It was new – it was singular – it was simple!" and, from admirals downwards, it was repeated – "It must succeed, if ever they will allow us to get at them! You are, my Lord, surrounded by friends whom you inspire with confidence." '

'The Nelson touch': it was a phrase he only used in his letters to Lady Hamilton, and probably it was a private joke between them.* But in after years, when his letters to her were made public, it came to mean two things: in general, his touch of genius and in particular the tactical plan he made before Trafalgar. To him and to her it meant the plan; for at those two dinner parties, he explained his thoughts and intentions to all the captains, assuming without any question that every one of them was competent and brave.

The plan was a revolution of naval tactics. Nobody made any record of his verbal explanation of it, but a few days later he sent

* As a pure guess, it might have started from the name of the French admiral at Toulon in the first year of the blockade, La Touche Treville, who made him extremely angry by writing in a letter that he had run away. Nelson had a copy of the letter – 'and by God, if I shall take him he shall *eat* it.' 'I will give him La Touche,' he might well have said then, 'La Touche Nelson.'

them all copies of a memorandum which summarized what he had said. The plan had evolved in his mind on the voyage to the Indies. During that voyage, in different circumstances, he had written another memorandum, and the preamble of it applied to both, and expressed the uncompromising confidence he gave to generations of British sailors: 'The business of an English Commander-in-Chief being first to bring an enemy's fleet to battle on the most advantageous terms to himself, (I mean that of laying his ships close on board the Enemy, as expeditiously as possible;) and secondly, to continue them there, without separating, until the business is decided –'

The Trafalgar memorandum made this same assumption: ships would be laid on board the enemy – that is, alongside and touching – and would stay there, and would win. But hitherto, fleets had always fought in formal lines of battle. Ships could only fire broadside: fore and aft, they had no guns, or few. So they manoeuvred in straight converging lines until each ship was in range of its opposite number, broadside to broadside. Victory then depended on separate individual duels of gunnery. But Nelson expected to have a fleet of forty ships, and expected the enemy to have even more. No day was long enough, he believed, to form so many into the usual line. So they would attack in three separate lines or divisions, one of sixteen ships which he would lead, another the same led by Collingwood as second in command, and an advance squadron of eight of the fastest sailers, which could be engaged where it was needed. Collingwood would cut the enemy's line twelve ships from its rear and overwhelm the rearguard, and he himself would cut it in the centre, where the enemy commander-in-chief would probably be. He did not specify what he expected to happen after the line was cut, but he had said in England, and undoubtedly said to the captains, that he wanted to bring about a 'pell-mell battle'.

The memorandum, in the clear unstudied language he always used, provided for attacks to windward or to leeward, and some passages summed it up:

'The whole impression of the British Fleet must be to overpower from two or three ships a-head of their Commander-in-Chief, supposed to be in the Centre, to the Rear of their Fleet. I will suppose twenty Sail of the Enemy's line to be untouched, it must be some time before they could perform a manoeuvre to bring their force compact to attack any part of the British Fleet engaged, or to succour their own Ships, which indeed would be impossible without mixing with the Ships engaged.

'Something must be left to chance; nothing is sure in a Sea Fight beyond all others. Shot will carry away the masts and yards of friends as well as foes; but I look with confidence to a Victory before the Van of the Enemy could succour their Rear, and then that the British Fleet would most of them be ready to receive their twenty Sail of the Line, or to pursue them, should they endeavour to make off . . .

'Captains are to look to their particular Line as their rallying point. But, in case Signals can neither be seen or perfectly understood, no Captain can do very wrong if he places his Ship alongside that of an Enemy.'

The novelty of this plan which so excited the captains was in dividing a single battle into three: two battles, more or less separate, would be fought simultaneously, and they would be won before the enemy van could turn in formation and try to begin the third. The fleet as a whole was outnumbered, but by this means each squadron would have the advantage of sixteen to roughly twelve. When the day came, Nelson changed the formations he had planned, because both fleets were smaller than he had expected, while the urgency of getting into battle was even greater. But the principle remained, and this was how Trafalgar was fought and won; and indeed one strength of the plan was that it could be changed, because every captain perfectly understood its basic intention.

But there was more than a matter of tactics in the 'Nelson touch', whatever he and Lady Hamilton may have meant by the phrase. There was also his unquestioning assumption that any captain and crew of a British ship-of-the-line would fight and beat whatever enemy ship they met. From his victories in the past, all the captains had confidence in Nelson: the confidence he showed in them made them also confident of themselves and of each other. And there was something further: the way he presented the plan, his blend of authority and friendship. Every captain who was there, and who left any record of his feelings, regarded Nelson as his personal friend. And they were right. Nelson liked people, and that was one reason why people liked him. But he did not like them indiscriminately. He liked them unless he had some positive reason not to, but when he disliked a man he did it thoroughly, and nobody was left in any doubt about it.

Collingwood was a man he had always liked in spite of his crusty manner. Now he had to be soothed. The general joy must indeed have been galling for him. Nelson wished him to move his flag from the Dreadnought which was barnacled and slow, to the Royal Sovereign, which had just been re-coppered in England. The change did not please him. He had worked up the Dreadnought's crew to a pitch of efficiency, and did not want to have to start again, and he asked rather petulantly about taking his officers with him. On the day after the dinner parties Nelson had a long discussion with him alone. Nobody knows, of course, what tactful words he used, but a few days later he sent a letter, which was a model of tact, with Collingwood's copy of the memorandum: 'I send you my plan of attack, as far as a man dare venture to guess at the very uncertain position the enemy may be found in: but, my dear friend, it is to place you perfectly at your ease respecting my intentions, and to give full scope to your judgement for carrying them into effect. We can, my dear Coll, have no little jealousies: we have only one great object in view, – that of annihilating our enemies, and getting a glorious peace for our country. No man has more confidence in another than I have in you; and no man will render your services more justice than your very old friend, Nelson and Bronte.' That friendship stood the strain.

And there was the problem of Calder. Calder had not been a

friend; long before, they had disagreed. But finding him now in trouble, Nelson did everything he could to mend the breach. Like everyone else in the fleet, he thought the criticism of Calder was ignorant and unfair; and what made it worse was that people at home had been saying 'If only Nelson had been there –.' It was a fact that Nelson's successes had set a high standard for any other admiral, but he was acutely embarrassed when people compared him with other admirals to their disadvantage. Before he left England he had said, as publicly as he could, that it was nonsense to assume that he or anyone else would have done any better than Calder. But now, he had brought a letter from the Admiralty, addressed to Calder, and he knew what it contained: an invitation to ask for a court of inquiry. He was very reluctant to send for Calder and present it; but at least, coming straight from England, he was able to tell him exactly what accusations he would have to face, and to offer him sympathy and a friend's advice.

Calder had to go home: the question remained of what ship he should go in. The Admiralty intended he should leave his flagship, the Prince of Wales, ninety guns, and take the Dreadnought, since she was due for docking. But this would have seemed a humiliation before the fleet, and almost a pre-judgement of the issue. Calder was desperately anxious to keep his own ship. Nelson hesitated, torn between common sense and kindness. From a strictly military point of view, it was indefensible to deprive the fleet of one of its most powerful ships, simply to help the self-respect of a single man. At first he must have refused, because Calder wrote to him: 'The contents of your Lordship's letter have cut me to the soul. If I am to be turned out of my ship, after all that has passed, I have only to request . . . that I may be permitted to go without a moment's further loss of time. My heart is broken.' This was too much for Nelson: when he believed a thing was just, he was often reckless of the consequences. He let the flagship go, and wrote to the First Lord of the Admiralty: 'I may be thought wrong, as an officer, to disobey the orders of the Admiralty . . . but I trust I shall be considered to have done right as a man, and to a brother officer in affliction – my heart could not stand it, and so the thing must rest. I shall submit to the wisdom of the Board to censure me or not.'

Whatever the Board of Admiralty thought, the captains off Cadiz thought Nelson was right. The whole affair had made a deep impression on them – the ingratitude, as they saw it, of people who could condemn a man at the end of a lifetime's service – and things were happier when Calder had gone and they could begin to forget it. But Nelson had not forgotten. 'What would poor Calder give to be with us now!' he said, as the first French shots went over at Trafalgar.

Somehow, in those three weeks, the confidence the captains felt spread right down through the ranks to the lower deck. Partly this may have been due to the captains' influence – such feelings can be infectious. Partly it was due to the legend Nelson brought with him. Very few of the seamen, except the Victory's people, can have seen him, but they knew very well what he looked like: they knew the empty sleeve from Teneriffe, the blind eye from Calvi, the scar on his forehead from the Battle of the Nile – such honourable souvenirs belonged more often to seamen than to admirals. And they knew the stories of the signal of recall he refused to see at Copenhagen, and of the two Spanish ships he boarded in person at the Battle of Cape St. Vincent. They believed he was a man to lead them into danger, not to send them.

And there were some small events that directly affected the people. 'What is the matter?' Nelson asked on one of those days off Cadiz, observing that his signal officer, Lieutenant Pasco, looked annoyed. A ship had just left with mail for England and was under full sail, already some distance off. 'Nothing that need trouble your Lordship,' Pasco said. But Nelson insisted, and Pasco told him: the boatswain who had loaded the Victory's mailbags had forgotten to put in his own letter to his wife, and had found it in his pocket. 'Hoist a signal and bring her back,' the admiral said; 'who knows that he may not fall in action tomorrow?' And the ship returned, and hove to while a boat was launched to carry the single letter. Stories like this went quickly round the fleet, and were gratefully remembered: old sailors, years afterwards, told them to their children. Of course it was not very hard to seem kind to men who seldom received much kindness. But it is always a delicate balance to be kind and yet to maintain a standard of discipline, and especially delicate for a commander-in-chief to be kind to the lowest ranks of men without undermining his officers' authority; and most delicate of all when the discipline is harshest. Nelson succeeded because his kindness was inherent. 'Men adored him,' a sailor simply wrote, 'and in fighting under him, every man thought himself sure of success.'

No seaman's pride in his ship or his calling was ever very far below the surface: only inhuman treatment or utter boredom could suppress it. By Nelson's coming it was passionately roused. In those three weeks, each ship could be seen with bosun's chairs slung overside and scores of sailors scraping and painting. Before the day came, all of them wore the yellow bands and black gunports Nelson had chosen for his Mediterranean fleet.

All these matters of human relationships must have taken a lot of Nelson's time, but perhaps not much of his thoughts: he only behaved in the way that was natural to him. His thoughts were absorbed by the problem of bringing the French and Spanish to battle.

Collingwood had lain with his ships in sight of the land, and no doubt he was right to do so until the fleet was strong enough to fight. That was the policy at Brest, where he had come from: to keep the enemy in. But Nelson returned to the policy he had pursued at Toulon: to tempt them out. It had failed there, because when they did come out he lost them, and he ran a risk of losing them again. But, like everybody else, he could hardly bear the thought of another winter out there, and he longed to get it over in a final annihilating fight.

Nobody knew if the French still meant to head for the Channel or – another danger – to try an invasion of Ireland. Nelson believed they would go for the Mediterranean, and try to get back to Toulon. For the Channel or Ireland, they would have to round Cape St. Vincent, a hundred and fifty miles west of Cadiz: for the Mediterranean, to pass the Strait of Gibraltar, sixty miles south. He stationed the body of the fleet fifty miles west-south-west of the town, far enough out to be sure they would not know where he was, and far enough, if they guessed, to give them some hope of escaping in either direction. To watch them, he sent his squadron of frigates close inshore, where they could see the crowd of masts inside the harbour, and between the frigates and the fleet he stationed a row of ships to relay signals. To prepare for a long wait, he decided to send the ships five at a time to Gibraltar for stores and water, and to Tetuan, which was a port for beef. On October 3rd the first five left the fleet, but between the 7th and 14th five more ships joined from England, bringing his numbers to twenty-seven of the line.

Meanwhile, rumours were coming out of Cadiz, through Gibraltar and from Portuguese fishermen, of what was happening there. Some of them said the French and Spanish fleets were starving, and some that Napoleon had ordered them out and they had held a Council of War and refused to go. Some said the admirals had been recalled to Paris, and some that the French commander-in-chief had been dismissed. None of these rumours were true, but there was a little truth in all of them.

CADIZ

Admiral Villeneuve, in Cadiz, was a lonely, unhappy man. He was young to have reached so high in his profession, only 41. Ships were his life and his home, and in the splendour of the admiral's cabin of the *Bucentaure*, surrounded by a fleet at his command, he deserved the satisfaction of fulfilling a high ambition. But its fulfilment had brought him nothing except confusion and petty conflict. Enemies, some open and some secret, were crowding in on him, inevitably driving him towards disgrace, despair and melancholy death.

Pierre Villeneuve was an officer who had entered the navy as a boy and made a life's career of it. In France, there were none too many like him. Before the Revolution, the navy had been a profession for the gentry, as it was in England, and also for the aristocracy; and consequently, during the Revolution, a great many officers had been executed or driven into exile. Villeneuve had escaped the fate of so many of his friends because he sincerely believed in the Revolution; and in the shortage of officers afterwards he had quickly been promoted. He was rear-admiral when he was 32; but since then, he had never had much success. He had taken part in the expedition to Ireland in 1796, which ended in disaster, and he had escaped – ignominiously, some people said – from the worse disaster of the Battle of the Nile.

Villeneuve had one fundamental misfortune he shared with the whole of the navy: he was fighting for an Emperor who was a soldier, not a sailor. Napoleon was accustomed to order his army to do what seemed impossible, and under his direct command the army often did it. But his orders to his navy sometimes overstepped the mark: knowing too little of the sea, the genius faltered, and he demanded what was really impossible. When his admirals tried to explain, he grew angry, and accused them of trying to hide their cowardice or inefficiency behind their technical terms. Villeneuve had believed, ever since he had been appointed at Toulon, that his orders were one of these impossibilities: a French navy, whatever it did, could not win command of the English Channel. At the beginning he might have refused the appointment, but he had let himself be tempted by promotion; and ever since, the thought that he could not carry out the Emperor's grand design had made his command a nightmare. Ganteaume, Missiessy, and even Decrès the Minister of Marine, would all have agreed with him. But none of them dared to tell the Emperor plainly; and Villeneuve could not bring himself to sacrifice his ships and men in a brave but hopeless attempt. So, whenever a crucial moment came, he hesitated, and in the fleet, among men who were less clear-headed and well informed than he was, the whisper spread that the admiral was afraid.

He was not afraid – at least, not for his own skin: he was a realist. Perhaps he knew in the back of his mind that a nation which had killed or driven out its naval officers could hardly hope for victory at sea. Certainly he knew that ship for ship and man for man, the French were no match for the English, and he knew above all that he was no match for Nelson. The weakness of the fleet had been shown in an abortive sortie from Toulon in January, when stormy weather had driven him back to port. 'The fleet had looked well in harbour,' he reported on that occasion to Decrès the Minister, 'but in the gale things were very different. The few sailors were lost among the soldiers, who were seasick and could not remain in the batteries but encumbered the decks. It was impossible to work the ships. Spars were broken and sails carried away, as much by clumsiness and inexperience as through bad materials supplied by the dockyards.' Yet Nelson's fleet, he knew, had weathered that same storm, thought nothing of it, and still remained fighting fit at the end of it. The Emperor, it was said, believed his fleet could be conserved in port, while the English were wearing themselves out at sea. But the opposite was true. Neither Villeneuve nor any other admiral could make good gunners or seamen, or even good signallers, midshipmen, pursers or doctors, without the open sea to train them in. And Villeneuve's fleet, whenever it should have been training, was unable to put to sea without the immediate risk of battle against a fleet already perfectly trained. Even the voyage across the Atlantic and back had been too hasty for training: there was no ammunition to spare for gunnery practice. It had not improved the fleet; it had only shown up its weakness. Most of the ships had come back in need of repair, and some with a third of their crews out of action through illness. And Nelson's, it seemed to him, had come back as fit as ever, and was still at sea, still eagerly waiting outside his harbour like a cat outside a mousehole.

Yet Nelson was not Villeneuve's worst enemy: inside the harbour he had others. If he had not been a Frenchman, Nelson might well have been his friend. He was first and foremost a professional officer, and he could have felt at home in the other fleet: among Nelson's professionals, and under Nelson's leadership, he could have been one of what Nelson sometimes called the 'band of brothers' – and indeed, when they captured him, they found him a very English kind of Frenchman, which no doubt was the highest compliment they could pay. But in his own fleet, there was no band of brothers: he lacked the personality or the conviction to create one. Some of his captains were efficient, some seemed to be loyal to him, and a few were eager for a fight. But, also, some were plotting against him, and some were utterly discouraged by the endless demoralizing need to avoid a battle. It was a fleet at war within itself.

For this unfortunate man command of the fleet had been hard enough in Toulon: in Cadiz, it became much harder. He fell ill and suffered painful colics, perhaps through worry: for here he was in a foreign country, far from home, with nobody to turn to for advice or sympathy. He knew the Emperor would blame him for wrecking his grandest plan, and it was too late to say the plan had been impossible from its inception. He wrote again and again to his Minister Decrès, explaining what he had done and why he had done it, and describing the difficulties he was facing and what he was trying to do to overcome them; and one must imagine he waited in constant fear of a letter back from Paris. Week after week he was kept in suspense, expecting the Emperor's wrath; and the Emperor's wrath, with good reason, was dreaded by every Frenchman.

Meanwhile, against imponderable opposition, he struggled to make his fleet ready for sea again. He had eighteen French ships-of-the-line, and in his reports to Decrès he could only claim that five of them were fit in all respects. Others had inefficient crews, or needed to be docked to have their bottoms scraped or re-coppered; one had a damaged mizzen-mast, and one, the *Swiftsure*, was leaking six inches an hour. Most of them were short of sails and cordage. Of men, he had one thousand seven hundred sick, one in six of his total: he had put them ashore in a temporary camp. And three hundred had deserted since he left Toulon.

For every kind of help he had to depend on the Spaniards, and they were unwilling allies. Spain had a longer and prouder tradition of seamanship than France, and was well aware of it: so Spanish officers resented French command. And, unluckily, the only two ships that were lost in the fight against Calder had both been Spanish, and had both been manned in Cadiz. Spaniards were saying openly that the French had treacherously abandoned them, and Frenchmen, stung to reply, made matters worse by saying the Spanish ships had been lost by their own incompetence. Antagonism grew so strong that French officers were publicly insulted in the streets, and French sailors assaulted in the dark alleys at night.

And Spanish officials, through the same ill-feeling, refused to give Villeneuve the stores and services he needed. He could not put to sea without repairs, or without renewing his food, and his boatswain's and armourer's stores: indeed, without food, he could not even exist in port much longer. But the arsenals of Cadiz were almost empty and the city and countryside were hungry, oppressed by the British blockade. There was hardly enough of anything for the Spanish fleet: nobody wanted to supply the French, and let their own ships go short. Villeneuve appealed to the French Ambassador in Madrid, and the Ambassador protested to the Spanish government. At last, the government ordered the authorities in Cadiz to give him what he needed. The authorities had to obey, but they did it grudgingly, quibbled over every item, and insisted on payment in cash – and Villeneuve had very little cash. He fought a daily, dispiriting battle against red tape and sullen obstructionism.

All this might have been easier for Villeneuve to bear if he had had anyone to confide in. But he knew what some of his officers were saying about him, behind the superficial respect they had to show to his rank. Even with his two rear-admirals, his second and third in command, he could never be at ease. Admiral Dumanoir, the senior of them, was younger than himself, only 35, and he was another professional aristocratic officer of the old régime: but he was said to be disgruntled and discouraged because he had been passed over when Villeneuve had been appointed to command. Admiral Magon, next in seniority, had a temperament totally opposed to Villeneuve's, a reputation for hot-headedness and daring. It was said that when Villeneuve broke off the battle with Calder, Magon was so angry with him that he shouted abuse, in the presence of his own crew on his quarter-deck, and threw at Villeneuve's ship, which happened to be passing, all the missiles he could lay hands on, including his telescope and wig, which both fell in the sea. The story was told in deadly seriousness by one of Villeneuve's most malicious critics and it may have grown in the telling. But clearly Magon was not a man his commander could confide in.

And the eighteen captains were divided in much the same way. The most clear-headed of them must have shared the admiral's opinion of the Emperor's plans. But this was not an opinion that could bind them together. To have discussed it at all, and agreed that the Emperor was wrong, would have been too close to treason. The hot-heads, on the other hand, undoubtedly did discuss what they regarded as the admiral's cowardice; and this they could do in an aura of patriotic respect for the Emperor's wishes. It was a classic divergence of opinion which had often occurred before in the history of warfare, and often occurred again. Given impossible orders, some men do what seems the next best thing, and live to fight again: others try to do what they are told, and more or less gladly die in the attempt. But few have to ponder the choice for month after month, alone.

By September 24th, after a month in Cadiz, Villeneuve was able to write to Decrès that he was ready and would sail again for the Channel as soon as the wind allowed him. Four days later a letter arrived from Paris. By then, he knew, the Emperor must know the worst. But the letter contained no instant dismissal, no threat of court martial, not even a mild rebuke. Instead, it brought a completely new set of orders, addressed to him in person and signed by the Emperor himself. He was not to attempt the Channel: at the first favourable opportunity, he was to take the whole combined fleet, French and Spanish, into the Mediterranean, land his French troops in Naples and finally return to Toulon. He was to capture any enemy convoys he met; and the word enemy, he was told in strict secrecy, was to include Russian or Austrian ships. Nothing could have delighted him more, or done more to relieve his mind. The impossible plan was abandoned, he was given a second chance; and even with a clumsy, ill-trained fleet, the new task was inside the bounds of possibility. To reach the Mediterranean was a very different matter from trying to reach the Channel. The Strait of Gibraltar was not very far away: with a good north-easterly wind, there was a chance of creeping down unseen by the enemy, perhaps in a single night.

He must have been mystified too. He could not have guessed

what had happened: that the Emperor had lost interest in the all-important invasion, and abandoned it before he knew that his fleet was in Cadiz.

Villeneuve had put in to Cadiz on August 22nd. His letter confessing it reached Paris on September 1st or 2nd. On August 22nd also, the Emperor sent him a final optimistic order to come up Channel; it was written in Boulogne and sent to Brest. For a few days more, the Emperor waited at Boulogne, expecting to see the sails of his fleet. But on the 27th he ordered the army there to break camp and march towards the Rhine, and he launched the campaign in the east which led him to the triumph of Austerlitz. Within those few days something happened to make him admit to himself that the invasion was impossible, at least until another summer came. Nobody knows precisely what it was. The fleet was late, and the winter was coming on: his spies had reported Nelson was back from the Indies: events in the east were growing in their menace. For some such reasons, he suddenly made the decision. The French historian Edouard Desbrière wrote: 'Although events were to justify the marvellous intuition the Emperor showed at this critical moment, no more serious decision can ever have been taken on less solid grounds.' But this was the fact: he abandoned the invasion while Ville-neuve and Ganteaume, for all he knew, were fighting their way up Channel. And if Villeneuve had sailed to Brest, and done what he was told, he would have arrived off Boulogne to find the army gone – and would never, in those circumstances, have fought his way out again.

On September 1st the Emperor left Boulogne for Paris, and on that day or the next a courier brought him the news that Villeneuve was in Cadiz. So the news, when it came, was not entirely unwelcome: better a navy intact in Cadiz than fighting a battle, now useless, in the Channel. And by then, in any case, he had put the failure of the invasion out of his mind: he was engrossed by the new campaign – a straightforward land campaign which needed no help from the navy. He was sick of the navy. As for Villeneuve, he could not even bother at first to send him a reprimand. Decrès tried to justify himself and Villeneuve, and the navy in general. 'Until you have thought of something convincing to say,' the Emperor replied, 'kindly do not mention to me this humiliating affair, or remind me of that cowardly person.' And his new order to Villeneuve can only be explained by his scorn and anger. It reduced the navy to a role of transport for the army. Thirty-three ships were to run the gauntlet of the British fleet, with no other tangible purpose than to land about four thousand soldiers on the far right flank of his new and glorious advance.

The new order may have been given in scorn, but Villeneuve received it as a mark of confidence. For the next few days he was a man reprieved. 'I look forward eagerly,' he wrote to Decrès, 'to the moment when I can undertake the new mission entrusted to me – to a favourable wind for getting the fleet out of harbour, and to some chance of being able to escape the infinitely superior forces of the enemy, or at least of only having to fight against forces if not inferior then equal to our own.'

He also wrote a general order to the fleet. It was pathetic in its pretence of hope; and it was also, one must add, an example of the deceit commanders practise to instil false confidence in their men. 'Troops will be re-embarked on Monday next, and the fleet will sail immediately afterwards. Commanding officers will deduce from the position and strength of the enemy force before the port that a battle is likely on the day of sailing. The fleet should view with satisfaction the opportunity it is offered of showing that character and daring which will ensure its success, avenge the past injuries done to its flag, and defeat the tyrannical domination of England on the seas.

'Our allies will fight with us, under the walls of Cadiz and under the eyes of their fellow citizens: the gaze of the Emperor is fixed upon us . . .'

These brave but hollow words could not have carried conviction to anyone but his most ignorant sailors. Perhaps the resolution to do or die pleased men like Admiral Magon. But it greatly alarmed the Spaniards. Aware of fresh doubt and dissent, Villeneuve called a Council of War. It met on October 8th, on board the *Bucentaure*. Villeneuve, as commander-in-chief, took the chair: six French and seven Spanish officers were summoned to attend.

To judge by unofficial reports of that meeting, half-hidden mistrust and enmity came into the open: tempers flared, and swords were almost drawn. Villeneuve read out the Emperor's new order, omitting the secret instruction about the Russians and Austrians. The Spaniards protested. It was better to wait, they said: they knew the local weather, and predicted a storm: the English fleet could not stay where it was for ever. Above all, their crews were not ready yet.

This last excuse was painfully true, and Villeneuve already knew it was. The Spaniards had some excellent ships, but nothing like enough trained men for them. In sheer numbers, their crews were enormous – eleven hundred men in ships which the British or French would have manned with six or seven hundred. But to make up these numbers, their press-gangs had gathered in every convict and beggar from miles around, and army units had been drafted wholesale. It was said that not one man in ten was a seaman. Thousands of them had never been on board a ship before. Army artillerymen were manning the naval guns.

To all their objections, French officers answered sarcastically: a Spanish commodore, with his hand on his sword-hilt, had to be restrained from challenging Admiral Magon to a duel. Villeneuve, it was said, seemed greatly upset at the scene.

But it was he himself who next aroused the Spaniards. Something he said offended their sense of honour, and Federico Gravina, their senior admiral, rose in anger. Only a madman, he said, would think of putting to sea: the barometer was falling. 'It is not the barometer, but the courage of certain people,' Villeneuve replied with less than his usual courtesy. At that, the whole simmering resentment about the fight against Calder broke out afresh. A Spanish captain made an impassioned speech, opposed any joint action whatever with such allies as the French, and refused to sit down in the uproar he created.

But whatever scenes of discord there may have been, the Council managed to produce a unanimous minute of its meeting. 'All present recognised that the ships of the two allied nations are for the most part badly armed, through the weakness of their crews; that many of them have not yet exercised their crews at all at sea . . . and that the enemy fleet in the offing is much more powerful than ours . . . All are therefore agreed to wait for the favourable moment mentioned in the orders to the Admiral, which may arise if the enemy fleet is driven off by bad weather or obliged to divide its forces.'

This was much nearer the Spaniards' wishes than Ville-neuve's: all he gained from the Council was an agreement to move the fleet to the harbour mouth, so that it could sail at the shortest notice. He sent the report to Decrès. 'I cannot refuse to listen to the opinions that come to me from every side – that our forces are inferior to the enemy's, that to sail in such circum-stances would be an act of desperation . . . that a battle would be inevitable as soon as we left port, and that it would be blindness to hope for a favourable result with crews like ours, and particularly those of His Catholic Majesty . . . Nevertheless, I beg Your Excellency to assure the Emperor of the eagerness with which I shall seize the first opportunity to execute his orders.'

And in the same letter, he made a practical suggestion: that the fleets at Cartagena and Toulon should sally forth to create a diversion which would force the English to divide their fleet. This, he pointed out, could only be done by the Emperor's authority.

But the Emperor's gaze was not fixed on the fleet. On the contrary, he was in Austria by then, a thousand miles away, brilliantly directing his army towards the Battle of Ulm, and sparing no thought for the ships in Cadiz or the orders he had given them.

*

The cruellest blow of all was yet to fall on Villeneuve. His most vicious enemy had been a man he may never have suspected: General Alexandre Lauriston, who had commanded the military forces in the fleet and had sailed with him in the *Bucentaure*. General Lauriston may have had redeeming qualities in life: what he left to history was a record of the meanest treachery. Villeneuve did not communicate directly with the Emperor: his position obliged him always to write to Decrès. But Lauriston did. He was under Villeneuve's command, but he was also an aide-de-camp to the Emperor, and he used that position to send the Emperor secret letters which blackened the admiral's character.

The most damaging of these letters was written as soon as the fleet dropped anchor in Cadiz. There were pages and pages of libel. Lauriston, it seemed, had taken it on himself, when he was first appointed in Toulon, to complain to Decrès about something Villeneuve had said or done. Decrès had supported the admiral, and ever since then, Lauriston said, the admiral had 'behaved towards him with arrogance and conceit, and been unwilling to accept advice or counsel'.

No wonder: Lauriston was a soldier, but by his own account he insisted on telling Villeneuve what to do at sea, and endlessly criticized his naval tactics. Now, in a spate of vituperation, he poured it all out to the Emperor, a long story of alleged incompetence, indecision and cowardice. Villeneuve, he said, was overwhelmed by fear of Nelson. 'Sire, permit an aide-de-camp of Your Majesty, who has always told you the truth and has no other ambition than to possess Your esteem, to represent to Your Majesty that this squadron needs a *man*, an admiral with confidence and zeal.'

All this was a travesty of the truth, yet it was near enough to the truth to be doubly dangerous. Villeneuve's conduct was not above reproach: he reproached himself. And among all Lauriston's personal spleen and outraged military pride, there was one accusation that was sure to catch the Emperor's eye. Villeneuve had reported, through Decrès, that he had left Vigo intending to make for Brest, and had only been driven back to the southward three days later by the threats of the enemy fleet and a contrary wind. But Lauriston told the Emperor this was untrue: Villeneuve, he said, had never intended to try to go to Brest, but had told Lauriston before they left Vigo that their destination was Cadiz.

This letter reached the Emperor the day after he had sent his new orders to Villeneuve. It finally exasperated him. 'Admiral Villeneuve has gone too far,' he wrote to Decrès. 'This is certainly treason . . . Villeneuve is a wretch who must be discharged with ignominy . . . He would sacrifice everything to save his own skin.' And a few days later he ordered Villeneuve's recall: 'As his excessive timidity will prevent him carrying out my order, you will dispatch Admiral Rosily to take command of the fleet, and give him letters instructing Villeneuve to return to France and account to me for his conduct.'

Villeneuve, in Cadiz, knew nothing of all this. Decrès did not tell him: he followed the Emperor's order exactly, and gave the letter of recall to Rosily. Lauriston was summoned to join his Emperor in Austria: 'General Lauriston,' Villeneuve reported, without any show of emotion, 'on disembarking from the ship *Bucentaure*, was saluted by eleven guns in accordance with the Imperial Decree on military honours.'

But rumours reached Cadiz. At first, Villeneuve was glad to hear them: the news seemed just what he wanted. Rosily was a senior admiral known for administration who had not been to sea for years: Villeneuve assumed he was coming to help him in his difficulties, and he looked forward to discussing everything freely with a man of long experience. But then, between the 15th and 18th of October, the rumour grew more specific. He heard that Rosily had reached Madrid and was delayed there by a broken carriage spring – and still he had heard nothing from Decrès. But his own officers knew: all were saying he was to be dismissed. 'The general rumour is that he, Admiral Rosily, is to take command,' he wrote. 'Of course, I shall be delighted to surrender first place to him if I am allowed to keep the second: it is due to his seniority and knowledge. But it would be too frightful for me to lose all hope of a chance to prove I am worthy of better fortune. Whatever happens, Sir, I can only explain your silence about Admiral Rosily's mission by the hope that I shall have been able to fulfil the mission confided to me at this moment, and whatever the difficulties, if the wind allows me, I shall sail tomorrow.'

Was he right in this last enigmatic sentence? Perhaps Decrès, his old friend, had neglected to tell him the news in the hope that he would have sailed beyond recall, and taken his second chance, before the letter of disgrace was handed to him. If so, he succeeded.

All great events can be said to have trivial causes, and if the spring of Rosily's carriage had been stronger, or the roads of Spain less rutted, the Battle of Trafalgar would not have been fought. For Rosily's orders differed from Villeneuve's. Rosily was given some discretion: if the enemy forces were too strong, he was told he could wait and make preliminary sorties with small squadrons, which would serve to train the fleet and wear the enemy down. But Villeneuve was given no such option: he only received an imperative order to sail. And when Rosily reached Cadiz, the fleet had gone.

On the 18th, the weather had been fine, and during the day the breeze crept round from west to south-east. That evening, at last, a light north-easterly breeze sprang up. It blew all night. At dawn the next morning, Villeneuve made his signal to sail. Almost at once the breeze fell again: a few of the leading ships were under way, but most were still at anchor.

All that day, in fitful breaths of wind, the clumsy crews tried to work their ships out of the bay: some launched their rowing-boats and towed the ships. By nightfall Admiral Magon was out with his squadron of seven ships and some frigates. And outside the harbour, impertinently close, he saw three English frigates making signals to others hull down on the horizon: one of them set all sail and disappeared to the southward.

These painfully slow manoeuvres, so clearly observed by the enemy, put an end to whatever hope there had been of avoiding battle. A day had been lost, and the warning had been given. But Villeneuve persisted. At dawn on Sunday the 20th, the remainder of the fleet got under way, and ship after ship emerged from the harbour into the open sea. The people of Cadiz filled the churches to pray for them, and crowded the walls of the city to see them go in the wan October sunshine. Undoubtedly every captain knew the fleet was doomed.

APPROACH

The English frigates Admiral Magon saw were the Euryalus and Sirius, together with the sloop Weazle; and they were so close inshore when the dawn was breaking, that a midshipman named Hercules Robinson, on watch in the Euryalus, could see the ripples on the beaches of Cadiz and smell the morning freshness of the land. Every day, beyond the spit of land on which the city stood, they had seen the masts of the French and Spanish fleet, standing as thick as a wood. That morning, to their delight, they saw the topsails hoisted and unfurled.

Everything was ready for this moment. At sea, a line of other frigates extended to the outlying ships of Nelson's fleet, each within sight of the next. Before the sun was up, the Sirius hoisted twenty-six signal flags: 'To Euryalus – Enemy have their topsails hoisted.' And at seven o'clock a second group of three, the figures 370, the coded message 'Enemy ships are coming out of port.' At 7.20, Euryalus signalled Phoebe, standing out to sea: 'Repeat signals to look-out ships west,' and she added the all-important figures 370. Ten minutes later, Euryalus signalled Weazle and a schooner called Pickle to come within hailing distance: Captain Blackwood, the senior officer of the frigates, told them to take the news to Gibraltar and Tetuan, and to any ships that might be cruising off Cape Spartel. At 8.40, as they drew away, he signalled two more instructions to them: 'Make all possible sail with safety to the masts,' and 'Let one reef out of your topsails.' Magon observed the departure of the Weazle, but the Pickle was very small and he did not see her, or did not trouble to report her.

By that time, the figures 370 were passing along the line of ships towards the fleet, forty-eight miles away beyond the western horizon: Phoebe to Naiad, Naiad to Defence, Defence to Colossus, Colossus to Mars.

Early that morning, Nelson also made a signal and wrote a letter. The letter was to Collingwood: 'What a beautiful day! Will you be tempted out of your ship? If you will, hoist the Assent and Victory's pendants.' And the signal invited several captains to dine with him, among them Captain Cooke of the Bellerophon. Cooke signalled his acceptance, and the Bellerophon made sail and left her place in the line to approach the Victory, so that she would be close to her by dinner-time. However, the Bellerophon's first lieutenant was a young man called William Cumby, who prided himself on his eyesight. He was watching the Mars. She was so far away that only her topgallant masts were showing above the horizon; but at her masthead he saw flags, and he read them as 370. He eagerly

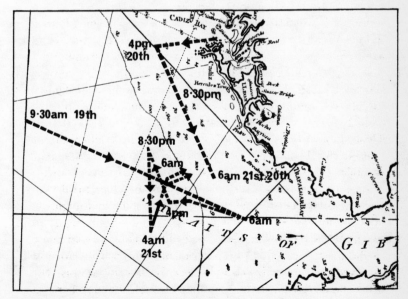

The approach to battle (superimposed on a chart of 1795)

told his captain. Captain Cooke looked through his telescope, but the distance was so great that he could not distinguish the colours of the flags: unless he could read the signal himself, he said, he would not repeat it to the Victory. Cumby respectfully insisted he was right, and persuaded Cooke to agree that if anyone else could read it, he would repeat it. Most of the officers and signalmen in the ship trained their glasses on the Mars, but none of them were certain what it was. Soon after, the Mars hauled down her flags. 'Now she will make the *distant* signal 370,' Cumby said. That was a combination of a flag, a pendant and a ball hoisted at different mastheads, for use when the colours of flags could not be seen. And within a few minutes up it went. The signalmen of Bellerophon hurried to hoist their flags, to be the first to tell the admiral the news he was longing for: but before they could do it, the Victory signalled her acknowledgement to the Mars. It was 9.30. Nelson had been told the enemy was sailing before the first of Villeneuve's ships had cleared the harbour mouth. He hoisted flags to cancel the invitation to dinner: and when they were hauled down, he signalled 'General chase', and ordered a course of south-east, towards the Strait of Gibraltar.

The system of signals they used was new, and it still seemed almost miraculous to be able to speak so quickly at such distances. The system was devised by an admiral named Sir Home Popham, and it had only been introduced in 1803. It was very simple. There were large coloured flags or pennants for the numbers from 0 to 9, and for a few important words, such as points of the compass. The same flags were used for the letters of the alphabet, from 1 to 26. And each ship had a code book, in which common words and phrases were allotted numbers from 26 upwards. If possible, ships used the standard phrases: 370, 'Enemy ships are coming out of port', was one of them. The next best thing was to use words which were in the code book. If any other word had to be used, it had to be spelt, the letters from A to I requiring one flag each, and the others two. The flags were hoisted to the upper yardarms or the mastheads, wherever they could be seen by the ships they were addressed to. Sometimes a message needed a great many flags, which gave the signalling ships an appearance of decoration. And sometimes signalmen made mistakes. The next signal from Euryalus that morning, at 11.05, was 'Nineteen under sail all the rest top yards hoisted except (rear steady) admiral and one line of battle ship.' This required fifty-six flags, and must have been sent in several separate parts: the words rear and steady were hoisted the wrong way round, and steady was a mistaken group: it should have read 'Spanish rear admiral'. But it was no wonder things went a little wrong: Hercules Robinson watched the signal midshipman and signalman sorting and hoisting hundreds of flags that morning, and thought they would die of it.

'Watch all points and all weathers, for I shall depend upon you': so Nelson had written, a fortnight before, to Captain Blackwood. Now was the time for that dependence, the time for the frigates to cling to the enemy fleet and signal its movements to the admiral – looking after themselves not by their gunpower, which was small, but by their speed, audacity and seamanship.

Blackwood was one of those small-boat captains who are found in every navy and in every epoch, the ancestor in spirit of the captains of motor torpedo boats. He was 35 and had been in the navy since he was 11, almost all of the time in frigates, and he had won a reputation, even in that age of expert seamen, of sailing them faster and more precisely than anyone else.

Oddly enough, he was a friend of Decrès, or at least a much-respected enemy, and he believed – and so did Nelson – that it was Decrès, not Villeneuve, who commanded the fleet in Cadiz. The friendship went back to a celebrated action off Malta three years before, when Blackwood in the 36-gun frigate Penelope, on a dark and stormy night, intercepted the 80-gun *Guillaume Tell*, the flagship of Decrès, and fought her single-handed until the morning. His method that night, which nobody else had ever achieved, was to come up close under the vulnerable stern of the bigger ship, then bring his frigate to the wind and fire his port broadside, then immediately wear her and fire the starboard broadside. To do that once would be a feat of seamanship, especially in the dark and a gale of wind, but he went on doing it all night, and so crippled the *Guillaume Tell* that English line-of-battle ships caught up with her in the morning and fought her to a standstill. Decrès was captured, and the two of them met and discovered a liking and admiration for each other. He was released at the time of the Peace of Amiens, and then was appointed Minister of Marine.

'What think you, my own dearest love?' Blackwood wrote to his wife that morning off Cadiz. 'At this moment the enemy are coming out, and as if determined to have a fair fight . . . I have time to write to you, and to assure you that to the latest moment of my breath, I shall be as much attached to you as man can be. It is odd how I have been dreaming all night of carrying home dispatches. God send me such good luck! The day is fine, and the sight magnificently beautiful. I expect before this hour tomorrow to carry General Decrès on board the Victory in my barge, which I have just painted nicely for him.'

Blackwood was also – it almost went without saying – a devoted friend of Nelson. They had not met before the Malta action: after it, Nelson as his commander-in-chief wrote him one of his irresistible letters: 'My dear Blackwood – Is there a sympathy which ties men together in the bonds of friendship without having a personal knowledge of each other? If so, (and, I believe, it was so to you) I was your friend and acquaintance before I saw you. Your conduct and character, on the late glorious occasion, stamps your fame beyond the reach of envy: it was like yourself – it was like the Penelope. Thanks; and say everything kind for me to your brave officers and men.'

And during the watch off Cadiz, Nelson's letters to him had been equally kind; from his station out at sea, he had written whenever a frigate or sloop could be spared to go to the inshore squadron. All of them, in Nelson's informal language, expressed his faith in Blackwood's judgement – the letters of a man equal in friendship though higher in command: 'I rely on you that we can't miss getting hold of them, and I will give them such a shaking as they never yet experienced: at least, I will lay down my life in the attempt.' And always there was a thought for the isolation of Blackwood's command, cut off from home and even from the company of the fleet: 'I send you two papers: I stole them for you.' 'There were no letters for you in the Royal Sovereign; at least, none came to the Victory. Collingwood has got the paper of the 23d; if he has not lent it, I have desired him to send it to you.' 'Send your letters – they shall be taken care of. Would you like them to go by Lisbon packet when I send mine?'

To Nelson's trust, Blackwood responded with his own self-confidence and skill. At noon, when the wind fell calm and halted Villeneuve part in the harbour and part out, the Euryalus also lay becalmed in full view of the city, hoisting elaborate signals: 'Notwithstanding little wind many of enemy persevere to get outward, the rest except one line ready yards hoisted.' That took upwards of sixty flags: the French could see them plainly, but could not decode them. At 1.50, there were over sixty more: 'Wind at present west. Enemy persevering to work outwards. Seven of line already without and two frigates.' The calm left the Euryalus helpless, drifting with the tide, but it must at least have given her seamen some rest. 'Made and shortened sail and tacked as the case required' was entered in Blackwood's log that afternoon when the wind had risen again: and that was an understatement of the labour of standing off and on in a square-rigged ship in light and variable breezes.

By dusk, twelve of the enemy were out: the Euryalus, under easy sail, was three miles away from them. 'Bore up and stood towards the enemy,' Blackwood noted, 'and observed the whole 12 standing towards the northward on the larboard tack.' Northward: this gave no indication of what they intended, they must in the end sail south for the Mediterranean or west for the Atlantic. All the evening he kept them in sight in the darkness, very close. But after midnight a sudden south-westerly wind sprang up and the sky clouded over, and he lost them. There was nothing in sight except the lighthouse of Cadiz, which was burning, and two unknown ships to windward, between him and the open sea. It was an anxious time, he said afterwards. Certainly this was a situation to make any seaman anxious – to be alone in the dark in shifting winds off a lee shore, among a hostile, invisible and vastly more powerful fleet. But the anxiety he remembered was only that the enemy might have escaped him.

That day and night Nelson took the fleet south-eastward, fretting impatiently at the feeble breeze.

The ships were only making three knots and the day seemed intolerably long. Men were aware that it might be the last day of boredom, perhaps the last of their lives: their thoughts turned to home. So did his. 'My dearest beloved Emma, the dear friend of my bosom,' he wrote, alone in his cabin at noon. 'The signal has been made that the Enemy's Combined Fleet are coming out of port. We have very little wind, so that I have no hopes of seeing them before to-morrow. May the God of Battles crown my endeavours with success; at all events, I will take care that my name shall ever be most dear to you and Horatia, both of whom I love as much as my own life. And as my last writing before the Battle will be to you, so I hope in God that I shall live to finish my letter after the Battle. May Heaven bless you prays your Nelson and Bronte.'

His dispositions were made, and until he reached the Strait of Gibraltar there was nothing more he could do. Surveying his line of ships, he could only see one detail he could improve. All of them had the iron hoops of their masts painted yellow, except the Belleisle, which had painted them black. He knew the French and Spaniards always had black hoops; so he signalled the Belleisle to paint hers yellow, and informed the fleet of this point of recognition, which might be useful when only the masts of ships could be seen above the smoke of battle.

The fine weather was one of the possibilities he had worried over. It was too fine. People who knew that coast better than he did predicted several days of calm and sunshine. Close to the shore, there would be a breeze off the land at night and a sea-breeze in the daytime. In those conditions he thought the French and Spaniards would use the breezes by coming out at night: then they might run down the coast and catch the westerly sea-breeze at the entrance to the Strait, while he was left with little wind in the offing. A third of the fleet was out: was the rest coming out in the darkness? He kept the Mars, Colossus and Defence out to port of the fleet, to maintain the contact with the frigates. Sir Edward Berry in the Agamemnon was also out on his own in that direction. The slowest sailers, Britannia, Prince and Dreadnought, were told to 'take station as convenient': he left them to lag behind. At dusk, he told six of the fastest to go on ahead, and to carry a light. Among these was the Bellerophon. Captain Cooke told Lieutenant Cumby that one of them should always be on deck until the enemy were brought to action or the chase was ended, and they agreed to stand watch and watch – a tiring arrangement, unusual for senior officers: they both hoped it would not last long.

All through that night, no more was heard of the frigates. They could signal in the dark: there was a limited night code, using guns and coloured lights, which could be used to give a rough idea of the enemy's course and position. So the absence of signals was alarming. Officers and look-outs, peering through the darkness, wondered what had happened. Were the frigates in trouble? Had they lost the enemy? Had the enemy fled into port again?

In twenty-one hours the Victory sailed sixty-five miles. When dawn came she had almost reached the mouth of the Strait, and the Bellerophon was six miles farther on. There was no strange sail in sight: the Strait was empty. The wind had changed to south-south-west – the same wind that Blackwood had experienced. It was raining, and squally. That wind would have headed the enemy fleet if it had been running down from Cadiz, and it put an end to the first of Nelson's worries: the enemy could not have got there before him and disappeared already to the east. It left three possibilities: either they were still coming, close-hauled among the rainstorms; or they were sailing west; or they were putting back to Cadiz. He wore the fleet and stood back the way he had come until eight o'clock, and then he hove to and called Collingwood and some of the captains on board the Victory. He was thirty miles south and west of Cadiz. The problem was to be close enough to catch the enemy, yet not so close as to frighten them back into port.

Villeneuve, in fact, was not in a mood to be frightened back, whatever happened. But he had not considered leaving the harbour in the dark. Cadiz had a bad reputation; one French fleet, not long before, had taken three days to get out of it. At night, it might have been done with a well-trained fleet, but with the Spanish crews it was out of the question. And Magon, already outside, had not gone far: after standing a little way to the north, his ships had hove to or anchored. Blackwood, in the light of dawn, was immensely relieved to find him still there, and the rest of the fleet inside, and getting under way. The frigates Naiad and Sirius were still on station, and from the masthead his look-outs could see twenty-two of the English fleet hull down on the southern horizon.

At 7.30 a strange sail came out of the north-east and approached Cadiz. Sirius signalled Euryalus for permission to chase, and followed the stranger in towards the harbour. Before she came up with her, both were in gunshot of the *Héros*, the leading ship of Magon's line of battle: the *Héros* bore up to bring her broadside to bear, and opened fire on the Sirius. But the Sirius, with the insulting disdain that was characteristic of the English at sea, took no notice: she fired a shot across the stranger's bows, and launched a boat to board her and inspect her papers. It proved to be an American merchantman that had chosen this awkward moment to visit Cadiz. Sirius, still under fire, waited for her boat, hoisted it on board again and leisurely set sail. Soon after, the American was boarded by the French.

Before that minor drama was over, another unexpected ship

hove into sight through the thickening rain: a large line-of-battle ship, towing a brig, which steered with all sail directly towards Magon's line and very close to it. It was Sir Edward Berry's Agamemnon. Blackwood watched her in astonishment: she seemed, incredible though it was, not to know the fleet ahead of her was French. He hoisted 'Enemy in sight north-east', and fired a gun to draw her attention. But on she went. He repeated the signal with seven guns before it was noticed. Then the Agamemnon hauled to the wind and tacked, still towing the heavy brig behind her. Next Blackwood made the signal 403, which was not in Popham's signal book and must have had some temporary meaning: perhaps it expressed his feelings.

But as the Agamemnon was there, he thought he would ask her to help. The weather was getting thicker. So far as he knew, she should have been with the fleet; he supposed she would rejoin it, and so he asked her to carry his information. 'Repeat signals to look-out ships,' he signalled at ten to nine: and twenty minutes later he had hoisted eighty flags: 'Seen thirteen ships without port, rest yards hoisted. Enemy cannot see English fleet. All the rest coming outward with expedition. Spanish commander chief coming outward.' He also signalled the course the Agamemnon should steer to find the Victory, which was south-south-west, and asked her to make all sail. But she stood on slowly towards the south-east, still towing the brig, until he lost sight of her.

The Agamemnon's behaviour is still a mystery. Perhaps Sir Edward Berry was not on deck so early in the morning. But her master was, and he evidently had very little idea of what was happening. 'Several strange sail in sight,' he innocently entered in his log. At eight o'clock he added: 'The Euryalus made signal of an enemy in sight.' And later, when the revelation had come upon him: 'Counted 30 sail of the enemy.' The brig was one she had boarded the day before: that afternoon she cast it off again, but there was no explanation of it in the log. And on her leisurely way to rejoin the fleet, a sudden squall carried away her main topmast, blew two sails overboard and split the mainsail. She stopped to repair the damage.

The same squally weather reached Cadiz just as the last of Villeneuve's ships was clearing the bay. About ten o'clock it started to pour with rain.

Among the squalls, at that important moment, Blackwood lost sight of the enemy fleet again. For two hours he tacked and changed sail, reefed and unreefed, searching for them through the drenching rain. And then in a sudden clearance he found them, almost on top of him, well within gunshot, sailing west. Before they could bring guns to bear, he wore* and escaped them. All this time, he must have been worried about the signal he had given the Agamemnon. Now he decided to take the news himself. He signalled to Sirius: 'I am going to the Admiral, but will return before night.' And he shook out his reefs and set topgallant sails, and made a southerly course to look for Nelson.

This was an example of what a frigate could do. The Victory was almost dead to windward, and almost thirty miles away. But in less than three hours Blackwood was in signalling distance of her. On his way, he saw the Agamemnon with her topmast down, but he did not recognize her, and perhaps it was just as well. To the Victory, he hoisted: 'The enemy seems determined to push to the westward. 30 north by east.' '30' was the number of enemy ships, and 'north by east' their bearing. Victory acknowledged the signal, and he wore to go back to his station. Before he lost sight of the English fleet he had the satisfaction of

---

* A ship is on the port tack when the wind is coming from its port or left side; on the starboard tack when the wind is from the other side. The verb 'to tack' means to alter course from one tack to the other, bringing the bows towards the wind. To wear is to alter course similarly, but bringing the stern towards the wind:

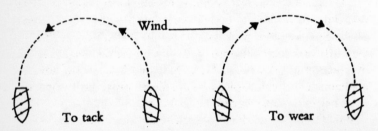

seeing the whole of it wear to follow him. And as he sailed away he read another reminder and reassurance which Nelson hoisted for him: 'I rely on you keeping sight of the enemy.' By four o'clock he was back with the French again. Some of them began to alter course towards him. It looked as if they were coming to reconnoitre the frigates, and he tacked to keep out of the way.

For Villeneuve, the shift of wind to the south-south-west in the middle of the night, when some of his ships were out and some were in, was the worst thing that could have happened. It was a fair wind for leaving the harbour, but foul for his course to the Strait. No admiral willingly put to sea when the wind was against him: the sensible seamanlike thing to do was to wait for the wind to change. But Villeneuve was driven by forces which overrode the simple decisions of seamanship.

Of course, he did not want to push to the westward, as Blackwood expressed it. But once he was out, there was nothing else he could do. A single frigate like Euryalus could beat to windward in short tacks. A single ship-of-the-line like Agamemnon could do the same thing, though more clumsily and slowly. But with a large fleet, short tacks were difficult and complicated, and apt to end in confusion. Once, through necessity, Nelson had tacked his whole fleet through the narrow Strait of Messina; but such delicate sailing called for far more skill than Villeneuve's ships could muster. He could only expect to make the Strait by a single long tack. With the wind as it stood when he started, that meant he had to be twenty or twenty-five miles off shore before he could turn and clear the shoals of Cape Trafalgar.

The squalls hit him as soon as he was in the open sea. He reefed the *Bucentaure* and signalled the fleet to do the same. Some of the Spanish ships took so long about it that they fell far to leeward, wrestling with torn sails. A man on the *Bucentaure* fell overboard, and the *Redoutable*, which was close astern, hove to and launched a boat to pick him up. Very slowly, one by one, his ships began to make way to the westward.

But suddenly, at four o'clock that afternoon, the wind

changed again. It flew round to the west. That was a wind abaft the beam for the Strait: he could tack at once, and he did so. For a moment it must have seemed that luck was with him. But even the single tack was as much as the fleet could manage. Some of the Spanish ships had not recovered from reefing, and were still to leeward. Others were taken aback by the change of wind and lost their steerage way. Those which had made the turn had to shorten sail to wait for the rest.

And something worse had happened. The ships had come out of harbour in no particular order, and just after one o'clock Villeneuve had made signal for a formation of three columns, with a squadron of observation out to windward. To his dismay, and the chagrin of his more efficient captains, the fleet was unable to carry out this order. It tried, but fell into a state of confusion from which it never recovered. The formation was far from complete when the sudden change of course upset it again; and even when darkness came, five hours after the order had been given, few of the ships were in their proper stations, none of the columns was complete, and the squadron of observation was still mixed up with the rest. It was not a fighting fleet; it was only a large unmanageable mass of ships.

Nobody alive today could manoeuvre a fleet of square-rigged ships, and so nobody has a right to be critical of the French and Spaniards: one can only have sympathy for them, forced out to sea before they were ready by the wounded self-esteem of the soldier Emperor. They had never sailed together as a fleet, and there were simply not enough of them who knew how to do it. To take formation, or to keep it, was much more subtle work than merely sailing a ship from port to port. It needed captains, masters and helmsmen who knew the feel of their own ship and the capabilities of the others, and it needed crews who at least could do what they were told, and do it quickly. It was not enough that some of them understood their business: they all had to understand it. A few ships unable to reach their stations made it impossible for the rest; and within each crew a few men who muddled their orders, cast off the wrong sheets or were slow in handling sails, could make havoc of what the captain was trying to do.

In the report he wrote when the whole disaster was over, Villeneuve said nothing about this failure to manoeuvre. Whatever his faults, he was what the English called a gentleman: he had reported his captains' shortcomings when they were in port, but once he had committed them to sea, he took the blame himself for all that happened. But several of the captains wrote about it; and the most outspoken of them was Captain Lucas of the *Redoutable*.

Lucas was an efficient, brave and fiery little man – the more fiery perhaps because he was under five feet tall – and he was extremely proud of his ship and his crew, as a good captain ought to be. While the fleet was in harbour he had trained his men in throwing grappling-irons and hand-grenades, and in musketry from the tops; and they had become so keen and proficient that they begged him to let them board the first enemy ship they met. That kind of training was only second best: naval battles were not won by musketry. What they really needed, like all the other crews, was gunnery practice, and that was impossible in harbour. But at least it gave them self-confidence – and it was to make its indelible mark in history.

Self-confidence was a quality Lucas never lacked. He was one of those men who emphasize their own efficiency by pointing to the inefficiency of others, and the fleet gave him plenty of scope for that unattractive habit. He was loyal to Villeneuve, at least on paper. The voyage could have succeeded, he believed, if only the other captains had carried out the admiral's orders – if only, in other words, they had been as efficient as he was. And that may have been true.

He was a boastful man. But to be a capable captain in an incapable fleet – this was a fate, one can understand, which was hard to bear with modesty and equanimity. Lucas and the others like him, watching the fleet's attempts at a naval formation, suffered a feeling of hopeless or furious frustration. And those unlike him, the ignorant inexperienced officers and men, suffered no doubt a hopeless bewilderment. At the bottom of this well of hopelessness were the thousands of men who had never been to sea and never wanted to go, and by now were lying below in the heaving dark confinement of the gun decks being seasick.

The feeling of frustration destroyed initiative. Nelson's captains felt their fleet was master of the sea: Villeneuve's felt theirs was beaten by it. While the Euryalus and Sirius were dodging in and out of gunshot of the enemy fleet, the French and Spanish frigates were lurking within the safety of their own. So the fleet was blind. Sailing into the gathering dusk that evening, it was only kept going by desperate bravery. The admiral did not know where Nelson was: in ignorance, the fleet was heading straight towards him.

Lucas's station was at the head of the centre column. From that position, soon after dark, he observed what he thought was a squadron or fleet, close to windward of him. It was making a great many signals which were meaningless to him but seemed remarkable for the beauty and brilliance of their coloured lights. He reported it down the column to Villeneuve: the Bucentaure was the fourth ship astern of him.

At the same time, seven o'clock, a different sighting was reported to Admiral Magon, who was out ahead of the fleet in his flagship Algésiras. A ship loomed out of the darkness and hailed him. She was the Achille: just before dusk, her captain shouted, her look-outs had sighted eighteen enemy ships to the south-south-west. Magon told the captain to find Villeneuve and make the report to him. He himself manoeuvred to approach Admiral Gravina in the Principe de Asturias, and shouted the news across from ship to ship. Gravina told the captain of the frigate Argus, and sent him also to look for Villeneuve.

This was another mark of the fleet's inferiority: by night, it had no method of signalling intelligence. The Achille had sighted Nelson's fleet before six o'clock, but it was half past eight before the *Argus* located the *Bucentaure*, and gave this vital information to the admiral. At once, he abandoned the formation in columns, and signalled to form a single line of battle. And fresh confusion began.

It was a very dark night, the wind was falling and a swell from the west was rising – which all made any manoeuvre more difficult. Even Captain Lucas, leading his column, was lost. He blamed the other captains. The admiral had made his signal with flares: so many other ships repeated it with identical flares that Lucas could not tell which of them was the flagship. The ships which were farthest to leeward, according to him, should have shown lights at their mastheads so that the rest could bear down on them; but if they showed any lights, he could not see them. He followed some other ships which seemed to be bearing down, but he could not identify them. After two or three hours of groping for position, he heard a voice which hailed him and demanded the name of his ship. It proved to be Admiral Gravina, who should have been leading the squadron of observation. Gravina was trying to form a line, and ordered him to join it. Shouting back, he asked permission to lead it, and Gravina agreed. And so he ploughed on, keeping course for the Strait. He did not know what the rest of the fleet was doing. But the decks of the *Redoutable* were cleared for action and he was satisfied she was ready for anything. He felt sure of a battle in the morning, and so he kept a minimum crew on deck and sent most of his men to turn in.

Perhaps they slept. But men on watch, all through the fleet, spent a night of anxiety and alarm. Lights and black shadows of ships showed through the darkness close at hand, and silently vanished again. Shouts came out of the night, demanding identities. Those who could see the stern lantern of a ship ahead clung to it, hoping it might be part of the line of battle. They should have hurried, to make the Strait by dawn, but they were only advancing at one knot and a half: everyone was under shortened sail, for fear of collision. The wind was still falling and the swell was still increasing, and the ships were rolling heavily.

And around them, to windward and ahead, the coloured lights of the enemy were burning up and fading, sending signals they could not understand. Sometimes guns were fired: they timed the flashes and the reports, and reckoned they were not two miles away. They had the uneasy feeling of being seen without being able to see.

All this alarm was self-engendered, or else was Blackwood's work: what Lucas took for a fleet or a squadron was only the English frigates, which followed the fleet all night like sheepdogs with a flock of sheep. They were outside the flock and could see it as a whole – or at least could see enough of its lights to know where it was and where it was going. Nelson was well out of sight. He had wore at half past eight and was standing south-south-east, on the same course as Villeneuve and fifteen miles ahead of him. He was keeping his distance, sailing away from the enemy, for he still thought they might put back to Cadiz if they saw him, and he did not know he had been seen before the darkness fell.

Twice in the night, officers in the Victory misread Blackwood's signals, and alarm was spread that the enemy had wore and was going back. But to wear a fleet in the dark was no easy matter, and if Villeneuve had wanted to try, it would probably have scattered his fleet irrevocably: even in Nelson's disciplined line, one ship, the Africa, missed the signal to wear and stood on to the northward alone. So Villeneuve crept slowly on, into the trap that was set for him. He could not do anything else.

'Up mainsail,' Blackwood wrote in his log that night, 'and kept upon the enemy's weather beam, about 2 or 3 miles. Made and shortened sail occasionally. Fired guns and burned false fires as necessary.' At midnight he could see the lights of both fleets. His job was done, and he went below and slept.

At 4.30 Nelson wore again and stood back to the north-north-west. The two fleets were approaching each other to meet at dawn. The Euryalus, which had brought them together, was still

in the middle, between the two rows of lights – like a cab in
Regent Street, as Hercules Robinson put it.

It had been a masterpiece of observation, signalling, seamanship and anticipation. When Blackwood awoke and saw that
battle was imminent, he finished his letter to his wife: 'The last
24 hours has been most anxious work for me; but we have kept
sight of them, and at this moment bearing up to come to
action . . . My dearest dear Harriet . . . Take care of my boy;
make him a better man than his father.'

BATTLE

Lieutenant Cumby of the Bellerophon, who had seen the signal from the Mars two days before, had spent a second night unwillingly standing watch and watch with his captain, and had only turned in at four o'clock. Just before six, the ship's master Mr. Overton shook him awake: 'Cumby, my boy, turn out – here they are all ready for you, thirty-three sail of the line close under our lee.' Cumby jumped up and put on his clothes again, and remembered to kneel down by his cot and pray for a victory, committing himself to God's wisdom and asking protection for his wife and children; and then he ran up on deck to see the enemy fleet.

In the next ship ahead, the Belleisle, a boy named Paul Nicolas was woken by the cheers of the crew and their footsteps as they pounded up the hatches to have a look. He was only just 16, but he was a lieutenant of Marines and second in command of the ship's Marine detachment. He rushed up too. The eastern horizon seemed to be covered with ships. Everyone was even more delighted, it seemed to him, than they were when they first saw the cliffs of England after a long foreign cruise.

Ahead of the Belleisle, the Tonnant: a midshipman on watch on the forecastle saw them first. As the dawn rose, he had been dutifully watching the ships ahead of him in line, the Mars and then the flagship Royal Sovereign; but he glanced towards the lightening eastern sky – and then eagerly ran to the quarter-deck to tell the officer of the watch.

The ships buzzed with excited talk, surprise, speculation, hope and bravado, and nobody tried to suppress it. Captains could

not afford to seem surprised, and most of them, understanding
Nelson's movements and the frigates' signals, probably half
expected what they saw. So they let themselves enjoy their
crews' surprise, like conjurers who had successfully produced a
rabbit from a hat. Collingwood, in his cabin in the Royal
Sovereign, asked his servant if he had seen the fleet. The servant
had not. 'Then look at them,' the admiral said. 'In a very short
time, we shall see a great deal more of them.' He looked, and
saw the crowd of ships; but he was much more surprised to see
the admiral calmly shaving himself as if it were an ordinary
morning. Collingwood finished and went on deck, where his first
recorded remark was addressed to his first lieutenant: 'You had
better pull off your boots and put on silk stockings, as I have
done. If one should get a shot in the leg, they would be so much
more manageable for the surgeon.'

Nelson, leading the line in the Victory, had been awake for
much of the night, but he was accustomed to that. He came on
deck soon after daylight, dressed in the same frock-coat he
always wore, which had the stars of four orders sewn on the left
breast. People noticed that he was not wearing his sword,
although he had always done so in other battles. He seemed in
the best of spirits, and told Captain Hardy that the 21st of
October had always been the happiest day of the year in his
family. Nobody knew what he meant and they did not ask him,
but afterwards they remembered that his uncle, who was a naval
captain, had fought a successful battle against the French on the
21st of October nearly fifty years before, in 1757.

He had already told Hardy, before he left his cabin, to hoist
the necessary signals to the fleet. The first, at ten minutes past
six, was to form the order of sailing. That needed little action.
The fleet with one exception had kept its order through the night
and only needed to adjust its intervals: the exception was the
Africa, which had missed the signal to wear the previous evening
and had stood on alone to the northward, and was now six miles
away. The next signal was 'Prepare for battle', and the third
'Bear up in succession on the course set by the Admiral.' The

Victory swung to the east-north-east, and half-way down the line the Royal Sovereign did the same. The others followed, and as they brought the breeze astern they set every sail, even the studding sails which were never normally used in battle because they were unhandy. Enthusiastically, they cleared the decks for action. In some ships, the enthusiasm was almost excessive at such a distance from the enemy: everything that was in the way went into the sea – but most sailors delight in any excuse to heave things overboard. The Belleisle recorded it all in her log: 'Threw overboard unavoidably, in clearing for action, butts in packs 7. Do., cut for grog and topsail halyard tubs, 2. Do., cut for cook's tubs, 3. Puncheons and harness casks, 2; some beef and pork in harness tubs, iron hoops, 6 parcels, 10 in each; biscuit bags from the different berths, 90 in number.' In the Tonnant, more frugally, they hoisted the Windsor chairs of the wardroom furniture on a rope between the main- and mizzen-masts, but some of them were shot to pieces there.

At 6.45 Nelson altered the course of the fleet to east: and that was the last manoeuvring signal he had to make, because everyone knew what to do. He said to Hardy: 'I shall not be contented with capturing less than twenty.'

To Villeneuve, the dawn showed an ominous sight: first, his own line of battle in fatal disorder; next, the shore of Cape Trafalgar, looming uncomfortably close to leeward; and then, directly to windward, the British fleet, which turned towards him, coalesced into two groups and set its studding sails, a sure sign of determination to close and bring him to battle.

His fleet was not unduly scattered. Thirty-three ships in line at the standard interval, which was 180 metres, would cover four miles of sea, and his fleet from van to rearguard was not much more than that. But it was not in line. The ships were in formless clusters with gaps between them, some were in double lines which masked each others' broadsides, and most of them were in nothing like the sequence he had ordered before he left port. Admiral Gravina, for example, had not yet assembled his

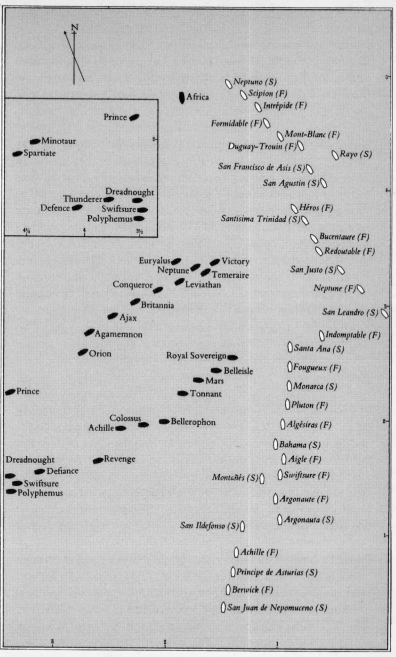

Noon: The Royal Sovereign opens fire

squadron of observation: about half of it was still mixed up with the other three squadrons. Captain Lucas, still leading the fleet in the *Redoutable*, was at least two miles and fifteen ships ahead of his proper station. The *Bucentaure* herself had the wrong ships ahead of her and astern.

In the early light, Villeneuve and his staff could not have seen how confused the sequence had become, and at twenty past six he hoisted a signal which was almost impossible to execute: form line of battle in normal sequence. This was substantially the same signal Nelson had hoisted ten minutes earlier, but there was a world of difference. To Nelson's fleet, it was not much more than a confirmation of the order they were in: but to Villeneuve's it meant a manoeuvre, a kind of general post, which with the best of skill and the best of conditions would have taken hours. And, for that purpose, conditions were almost as bad as they could have been: in the feeble breeze and the heavy swell abeam, the ships were rolling the wind out of the topsails, and were slow and uncertain on the helm. They tried. Lucas wore as soon as he read the signal, and sailed back to his station, three ships ahead of the *Bucentaure*, but it took him two hours to get there. Some others which were ahead of their stations did the same. But those astern of station could not catch up unless the rest of the fleet shortened sail to wait for them. The fleet already was moving very slowly – in the twelve hours from dusk to dawn it had made less than twenty miles – and it seems that this difficult manoeuvre brought it almost to a standstill.

While his ships were trying to disentangle themselves, Villeneuve was wrestling with the hardest decision of his whole career: to stand on for the Strait and the Mediterranean, or to put back towards Cadiz.

Nelson expected him to put back, and when some of the ships like Lucas's were seen to be wearing, he concluded that the whole fleet was doing so: at seven o'clock he wrote in his diary 'The combined fleet wearing in succession.' He held his course. The British fleet had the swell astern and the breeze on the port quarter, and so it was making better progress than the enemy. Nevertheless, the approach to battle was to be a long-drawn ordeal. The Victory logged her speed as three knots, but she can seldom have moved so fast: the distance between the fleets at dawn was estimated by some people as nine miles and by some as twelve, and it took the fastest ships six hours to cover it.

By seven o'clock, both Nelson's squadrons had begun to form in line astern of the Victory and Royal Sovereign, which were about a mile apart. This formation was not what he had foreseen in his memorandum, and it was often criticized in later generations – so often that the Admiralty appointed a committee, more than a century later, to investigate his tactics. It was a barren argument. It turned on the fact that he had drawn a little diagram in the memorandum which showed his own fleet in three lines, each parallel to the enemy's single line; whereas he led his fleet, when the day came, in two lines which were roughly perpendicular to the enemy's. The reduction from three lines to two was simple enough: both fleets were smaller than he anticipated. It was the attack in line ahead, instead of line abreast, which roused the criticism. Superficially, this was bad tactics, because it was bound to expose the leading ships, especially the flagships, to the broadsides of several enemy ships before they could bring their own guns to bear. Some people who write about history like to seem wiser than the people who made it, and ever since Trafalgar such people have implied that Nelson was foolish to take such an obvious risk.

These tactical arguments were confused because nobody who fought at Trafalgar drew a reliable plan of the battle. All the plans they drew were different, and all were drawn from memory. It was nobody's business to draw one on the spot; and even if somebody had tried, it would have been an impossible task for any one man, from any single viewpoint, to chart the positions of sixty ships, all moving, scattered over many miles of sea. Some people afterwards, in a mistaken defence of Nelson, tried to prove that Collingwood's division, at least, had attacked in more or less the position of the memorandum. And others argued that the attack in two lines ahead was not what Nelson ordered in his early morning signals.

His signal at dawn, in Popham's signal book, instructed the fleet to 'bear up in succession'. By the time the arguments were at their height, nobody clearly remembered what 'in succession' had meant to Nelson and his captains. Was it that each ship should sail on to the point where the admiral had altered course, and then alter course in his wake – which would preserve the formation in line ahead? Or was it that each ship should alter course as soon as the ship ahead had done so – which would produce a formation somewhere between a line ahead and a line abreast? Whatever it meant, the fleet that morning made a compromise. Nelson's division did its best to follow in his wake, though each ship cut the corner to close the gap ahead of it. Collingwood's division must have turned more quickly, for it finished the turn in an echelon, a column astern and somewhat to starboard of the Royal Sovereign. Both lines were irregular, but nobody cared. 'We scrambled into battle as best we could,' one officer wrote, 'each man to take his bird.' He was only a lieutenant, and tactics were not his business, but his phrase reflected the general eagerness.

Another thing confused this long-drawn argument: the clocks or watches in all the ships showed different times. Each ship had a chronometer for navigation which was checked by the sun every day at noon, but those were kept below deck, and officers making entries in the logs used their own pocket-watches to note the time, or estimated it from the sand in hour-glasses; and probably, in the excitement, their entries in the log books lagged behind events, and they guessed what the time had been. So the notes in the logs of different ships were hard to compare or reconcile, and the sequence of the day's events was full of anomalies. It is only in recent years that the logs have been carefully analysed, and the times reduced as nearly as possible to a standard. That work, and a comparison of all the eye-witness accounts, put it beyond any doubt that the attacks were made in two roughly formed lines ahead, and that this was what Nelson intended.*

To make his decision, he had to balance the finer points of an art that is lost and forgotten. Nobody nowadays has the knowledge to make the balance: all one can do is recall the considerations that must have been in his mind.

The memorandum gave the underlying reason for his tactics, and he expressed the same thought more concisely in a conversation shortly before he left home: 'No day can be long enough to arrange a couple of fleets, and fight a decisive battle, according to the old system.' In the open ocean, far from port, there might have been time for manoeuvre: the fleets might have stayed in contact through the night, and fought on the following day, broadside to broadside in the traditional manner. But every circumstance that morning cried out the need for hurry. In the light breeze, starting ten miles apart, it would take all morning to close the gap, even if the enemy did not try to run – and the breeze might fall or shift as the day advanced. If the enemy stood on towards the Strait, it would become a stern chase, and the French and Spanish ships, whatever their crews were like, were not more sluggish sailers than the British. But if the enemy turned back towards the north, as Nelson expected, there was their port of refuge in Cadiz, scarcely twenty miles ahead of them. On that course, the enemy would be close-hauled while the British had a quartering breeze, and there might be a chance to catch them – but only just, and only if the breeze held. To catch them, he had to sail straight at them: it had to be a head-on attack without a minute wasted, or no attack at all.

Foremost in everybody's mind, and especially in Nelson's, was the thought that this was the chance they had waited and worked for all through the past two years. In their eyes, it was a time for action, not for careful calculation of the risks. But the

* This analysis was made by Rear-Admiral A. H. Taylor in the 1930s, and published in the *Mariner's Mirror* of October 1950. The plans in this book are based on Admiral Taylor's.

risk could be calculated, and Nelson must at least have made a brief instinctive estimate.

The leading ships would be under effective fire from four or five enemy ships, perhaps two hundred guns, for the last thousand yards of their approach. As the breeze lay, it would take them at least twenty minutes to cover that perilous distance, and in twenty minutes some thousands of shot might be fired at each of them. In calm water, against experienced sea-gunners, it would have been impossible: the chance would have been too high that the ships would be crippled and stopped. But the French and Spanish gunners were not experienced at sea, as Nelson knew very well, and the water was not calm: whether the enemy fleet by then was sailing north or south, it would have the swell abeam and its ships would be rolling heavily. To aim from a rolling ship was the hardest test of naval gunnery.

There were two other causes, beside the lack of training, for the inferiority of the French and Spanish gunnery: one was technical and the other tactical, and Nelson undoubtedly also knew of them. The technical cause was that the French and Spanish still used slow-matches to fire their guns, whereas the British had flint-locks and only kept slow-matches in reserve for use if the flint-locks misfired. A flint-lock fired a gun almost instantaneously, so that a gunner could choose the moment on the ship's roll when his gun had the elevation he wanted. But a slow-match fired with a delay which could not be predicted, and in a rolling ship the elevation, and hence the range, was almost a matter of chance.

The tactical cause was that the French and Spanish were generally taught to shoot at their enemy's rigging, and they used a proportion of bar and chain shot, which was designed to cut spars and ropes. To shoot at the rigging showed a defensive attitude of mind: if it succeeded, it brought down the enemy's masts and stopped his pursuit. But the British aimed at the hull, and used nothing but round shot: their tactics, under the lure of prize-money, were always to try to capture an enemy ship with its masts and rigging more or less intact, so that it could be sailed

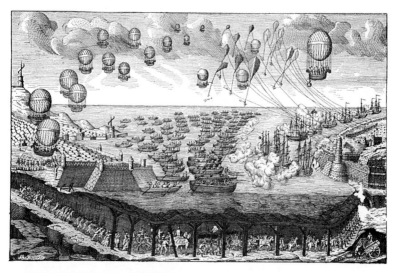

A projected idea for the invasion of England by sea, air and subterranean means from an engraving published in France in 1803.

The Victory at Sea by Monomy Swaine

Admiral Collingwood by Henry Howard

Sir Thomas Fremantle, engraving after
Bristow

Admiral Villeneuve, engraving after
E.Quenedey

Admiral Gravina, engraving after
Ramonet

Horatio Nelson,
Sir William Beechey

A portrait miniature of
Emma Hamilton which
Nelson kept in his cabin.
1800 by Schmidt

V. Adm.l Lord Nelson	Capt.n Bayntun		Capt.n Grindall		Capt.n Morris
Capt.n T. M. Hardy	Capt.n Codrington		Capt.n Hargood		Capt.n Bayfield
M.r Scott Sec.y	Capt.n J. Cooke	NAMES			Capt.n Pellew
L. Adm.l Collingwood	Capt.n Capel	of the	Capt.n G. Hope		Capt.n Rutherford
Capt.n Rotheram	Capt.n Digby	GALLANT HEROES	Capt.n E. Harvey		Capt.n Ashwell
R. Adm.l Lord Northesk	Capt.n Ham	who Commanded	Capt.n King		Capt.n Tyler
Capt.n Bullen	Capt.n Fremantle	on the 21.st Oct.r	Capt.n W. T. Lapenry		Lieu.t Clifford acting
Capt.n Sir E. Berry		1805.	Capt.n Hoorson		Lieu.t J. Stockham &c

POSITION of the COMBINED FORCES of FRANCE & SPAIN,

at the commencement of the Action 21.st Oct.r 1805 with LORD NELSON, Cape Trafalgar, bearing E.S.E. 4 Leagues

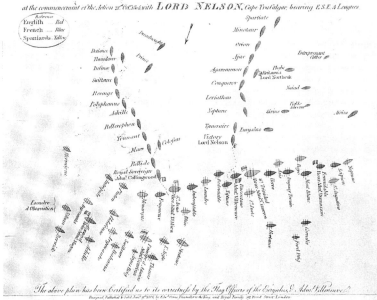

The above plan has been Certified as to its correctness by the Flag Officers of the Euryalus, & Adm.l Villeneuve

Designed, Published & Sold Jan.y 4.th 1806, by Edw.d Orme, Printseller to the King, and Royal Family, 59 Bond Street London

SUBSCRIPTIONS for a SPLENDID ENGRAVING of the DEATH of NELSON, SIZE 23 by 17.in are RECEIVED at 59 BOND STREET.

Nelson explains his plan of attack to his officers before the Battle of Trafalgar.

Wax effigy of Lord Nelson in the Westminster Abbey Museum

A page of Nelson's letter to Lady Hamilton, 19 October 1805

Victory Oct: 19: 1805
Noon Cadiz ESE 16 Leagues   125

My Dearest beloved Emma the dear
friend of my bosom the Signal has
been made that the Enemys Combined
fleet are coming out of Port, We
have very little Wind so that I have
no hopes of seeing them before tomorrow
May the God of Battles crown my
Endeavours, with success at all events
I will take care that my name shall ever
be most dear to You and Horatia both
of whom I love as much as my own
life, and as my last writing before the
battle will be to You so I hope in God that
I shall live to finish my letter after the

The Scene on the Deck of the Victory when Nelson Fell, by Denis Dighton

The Death of Nelson by A.W. Devis

After the battle: the Victory being towed to Gibraltar, after Clarkson Stanfield

Captain Hardy by Richard Evans

THE TIMES
For 7th NOVEMBER. 1805

BATTLE OF
TRAFALGAR

CAPTURE OF
FRENCH AND
SPANISH FLEETS

DEATH OF NELSON
List of Killed and Wounded

Poster made by street sellers with pirated copies of *The Times*. The news was not published until 7 November.

home and sold. To shoot at the hull with round shot could put
the enemy's guns and gunners out of action, but it seldom
wrecked the ship beyond repair. And when elevation was
uncertain, this method of shooting gave fewer misses. A shot
that went too high and missed the hull might still hit the rigging,
and round shot that went too low often ricocheted off the water
and did some damage. But by the French and Spanish method a
high shot went over the tops of the masts, and a low one, if it
were bar or chain shot, seldom ricocheted and seldom had the
power to penetrate the hull.

One must suppose that Nelson weighed all these considerations: the beam swell, the lack of training, the faults of
slow-matches and the habit of aiming high. Having weighed
them, he believed the Victory and Royal Sovereign, and his
other leading ships, would get through before they were
crippled. His captains all knew exactly what he was doing, and
what they had to do, and they did it without the slightest
hesitation.

In the hour after dawn, Nelson was not thinking of tactics:
probably he had decided it all in a moment. He was thinking of
home again, and no doubt most of the men in both the fleets
were doing the same. Soon after he came on deck, he went back
to his cabin and wrote what came to be known as a codicil to his
will. It was a strange and tragic document.

He had already provided in his will for his wife and the rest of
his family; but to Lady Hamilton he had left very little except the
house at Merton – the house which he and she and Hamilton
had agreed should belong to the 'longest liver' of the three. He
was not very rich, and nor was she, and since she was not related
to him she would not benefit from any pension, prize-money or
award if he were killed. Nor would Horatia, whom he had never
yet acknowledged as his own daughter. By changing his will he
could have provided something for these two people he loved,
but only by depriving his wife or his other relations, which he
might well have thought unjust: and so he wrote the unusual

codicil, which bequeathed not property but people. 'I leave Emma Lady Hamilton,' it said, 'as a legacy to my King and Country, that they will give her an ample provision to maintain her rank in life.' The reason he gave for this request was that she had rendered services to the State, while she was in Naples, which had never been rewarded, and he himself had been unable to reward. 'I also leave to the beneficence of my Country my adopted daughter, Horatia Nelson Thompson,' it continued, 'and I desire she will in future use the name of Nelson only. These are the only favours I ask of my King and Country at this moment when I am going to fight their battle. May God bless my King and Country, and all those who I hold dear.'

Very early that morning he had called the captains of all his frigates on board, and some time between seven and eight Blackwood and Hardy went down to the admiral's cabin and witnessed the document.

In relation to his services, the favours he asked were small, and he believed they would be granted: that belief was a comfort to him when he knew he was dying. And yet, it was only his strange innocence in such affairs that could have made him believe it. Other people, especially the King, were bound to see it in a different light: could a national hero be allowed to ask in effect for a pension for his mistress? No: when the question arose, the country provided lavishly for his relations and all their descendants, but gave nothing whatever to his lover, or to his only child.

While Nelson was occupied with that personal problem, Villeneuve had made his difficult decision. At eight o'clock, although his fleet was still in confusion, he signalled it to wear together and form the line of battle in reverse order on the other tack – that is, to turn and stand back towards Cadiz. On reading the signal, the Spanish captain of the ship which by then was leading the fleet, the *San Juan Nepomuceno*, said to his second in command: 'The fleet is doomed. The French admiral does not know his business. He has compromised us all.'

This angry comment has sometimes been quoted as a valid criticism of Villeneuve's decision. But it was not. On the contrary, Villeneuve was the only man on either side who had foreseen Nelson's plan of attack. In an order to his fleet, he had described so exactly the basic idea of Nelson's memorandum that some people afterwards thought he must have heard of it from a spy. It was true that Nelson had talked about it freely while he was in England, but it is hardly possible that the intelligence could have crossed the Channel and reached Cadiz so soon. And besides, Villeneuve had written a similar order months before, when he left Toulon. So he must be given the credit for remarkable tactical foresight.

He knew what to expect. At the time when he ordered the fleet to wear, his leading ships were clear of Cape Trafalgar and had reached a point where they could bear away for the Strait with the wind astern. From the *San Juan Nepomuceno*, the leading ship of all, this may have seemed the obvious thing to do, and with a ten-mile start she might have escaped to the Mediterranean. But the centre and rear of the fleet was not yet clear of the Cape, and frigates had told Villeneuve the English fleet was steering for his rearguard. If he stood on, the van of his fleet might be safe, but the rest would be overwhelmed: if he stood back, he would at least keep the fleet intact to meet the assault together.

Afterwards, he wrote that his only motive in turning back was to protect his rearguard. That was a sufficient logical reason, but one feels there must have been more in the back of his mind. It was not that he hoped to run back to Cadiz. From Nelson's distant viewpoint, that seemed a possibility; but, in fact, Villeneuve was already too close to the land. From the *Bucentaure*, Cape Trafalgar was bearing east-south-east, distant about twelve miles. From that position, in the existing breeze, with extra leeway caused by the onshore swell, it was scarcely possible that any ship-of-the-line could have weathered the shoals between Trafalgar and Cadiz and reached the port again without a tack.

To turn back as he did must therefore have been, at last, a

deliberate acceptance of Nelson's challenge. He had left port
without hope, and everything that had happened had made the
prospect of battle more hopeless still. All he had left was courage
and naval pride – and this, at least, he shared with his officers.

To the English, it certainly seemed the enemy were offering
battle – and doing it, as Blackwood said, in a handsome way.
Nelson had asked him what he would consider a victory. 'Con-
sidering their apparent determination for a fair trial of strength,'
he said judiciously, 'and the proximity of the land, I think if
fourteen ships are captured, it will be a glorious result.' Nelson
insisted on twenty, but he agreed it might be difficult to bring the
prizes off the shore.

There was never the slightest doubt of victory, only of how
extensive the victory would be. Throughout the fleet the feeling
was the same: mutual confidence had so pervaded it. But
nobody from highest to lowest can go into battle free from
doubt of his own survival; and that long morning, in which the
tension slowly rose to a terrifying inevitable climax, gave ample
time for private fear to grow. There was nothing for men to do,
nothing but wait and think. The decks had soon been cleared for
action, powder and shot were ready at the guns, crews stood
at their action stations. Most of them could not see what was
happening, unless they leaned out of the gunports, as they
sometimes did, for a glimpse of the enemy. Even on the upper
decks, the men stood idle. In the steady gentle breeze, and on the
constant course, there was seldom any need to trim a sail. All
was silent. The musical chord of the rigging had died away with
the wind, and so had the rush of seas alongside. The swell lifted
the stern of each ship in turn, pressing her on for a minute to a
respectable speed, and then passed silently under her to let her
fall back, almost without any way on her, into the trough. In the
Royal Sovereign, a young sailor was wishing he was at home on
his father's farm with his plough again. In the Belleisle, not far
astern of her, the officers were having breakfast, each wondering
who would be there for breakfast the following morning: one of

them openly said he thought he would be killed, and told the others how to divide his belongings. On the gun decks, men were making bargains: if I am knocked overboard, you can have my gear, and if you are I will have yours. And at breakfast in the Bellerophon, Captain Cooke gave Nelson's memorandum to Lieutenant Cumby to read, so that he would know what to do if the captain, as he put it, was bowled out. 'But possibly,' Cumby said, 'the same shot which disposed of you might have an equally tranquillizing effect upon me'; and they agreed to show the memorandum also to Mr. Overton the master.

It was nothing new for Nelson to think of his own death: it was one of his favourite topics of conversation. 'A peerage or West-minster Abbey!' he had said before the Battle of the Nile – just as his sailors, now before Trafalgar, were chalking 'Death or Victory' on their guns; and he was delighted after that battle when one of his captains gave him a coffin to be buried in, made from the timber of the French flagship *Orient*. He had often told Hardy what he wanted him to do with his body – to take it to England and bury it where he was born, at Burnham Thorpe in Norfolk, unless the country thought it proper to bury him at public expense. In that case he would prefer St. Paul's to Westminster Abbey, because he had been told when he was a boy that the Abbey was built on marshy ground and might in the distant future sink into it.

There was nothing morbid about this kind of talk: it was a healthy attitude of mind in a man who was sensitive and imaginative, and yet was always ready to die in battle: it regarded death as no more than a part of life. But in that long morning before Trafalgar, he seemed to go further in his thoughts: he seemed to expect his own death as certainly as he expected victory – so certainly that people have wondered whether he wanted to die.

To believe that would be too simple. But he was a man who long before had had to overcome all fear of death. And that day, one must suppose, he felt divided between his two loves, the love of Emma and the love of the men he worked with. Certainly, both loves were in his mind. He expected his victory would bring a peace to England, and if he lived he intended to go ashore for good, and settle down with Emma and Horatia, and grow old as a country gentleman. And yet, to achieve that ambition in peace of mind, the other love had first to be fulfilled. The fleet had demonstrated it, more clearly than ever before, since he came to Cadiz: they had set him on a pinnacle of trust. Their expectation could only be met by perfection in his conduct of the day. And in that light, all his actions can be seen to be inevitable. His own ship must be first in the line; he must be the most conspicuous figure in her, as he always was; he must pace his quarter-deck, as he always did, to observe and direct the business – not inviting death, nor doing anything whatever to avoid it, but simply accepting it if it came. It was likely to come: he knew it, and everyone knew it. But in his life he had set such a standard of heroic conduct, to himself, and to the fleet, and to the nation, that death in victory had become its only true fulfilment.

To live in Emma's love or to die in the ultimate vindication of his friends': if he was clearly aware of any choice, he believed the choice was not his. He went to his cabin again, a little later in the morning, and knelt at the table there, and wrote in a firm unhesitating hand his matchless prayer. 'May the Great God, whom I worship, grant to my country, and for the benefit of Europe in general, a great and glorious victory; and may no misconduct in any one tarnish it; and may humanity after victory be the predominant feature in the British Fleet. For myself, individually, I commit my life to Him who made me, and may His blessing light upon my endeavours for serving my country faithfully. To him I resign myself and the just cause which is entrusted to me to defend. Amen. Amen. Amen.'

Nine o'clock: the enemy fleet at five miles distance. Sombre thoughts were dispelled by an air of gaiety. The sun was well up, the sea was sparkling: the tension was relieved a little by music. Every captain who had a band ordered it up to the poop to do its best. Bands were a captain's conceit. Sometimes, they could be enrolled complete and ready to perform: Fremantle, before he left Plymouth, had been in negotiation for the band of a regiment of Militia which was being reduced, and he had imagined himself giving splendid entertainments; but the deal had fallen through and he went into battle without one, taking comfort in the thought of how much it would have cost him to provide the instruments. But other bands were composed of volunteers from the crew, who learned their art on board and played on drums made of barrels, triangles bent out of ramrods, and whatever fifes, oboes and bassoons they had managed to find in captured enemy ships. In the quiet air that morning, the bands could clearly be heard from ship to ship. They were all playing different tunes, some badly and some well, but the general effect was cheerful.

Every captain made his rounds as the morning wore on: so did Nelson and Collingwood, inspecting each deck, stopping to talk here and there to the captain of a gun, commending the junior officers on their readiness. Here could be seen the whole contrast between the ranks of the navy, and the strata of society: the men stripped to the waist, barefooted, with kerchiefs tied round their heads to protect their ears from the blast of the guns – and the officers dapper and elegant in frock-coats with epaulettes, immaculate silk breeches and stockings, and silver-buckled shoes. The contrast itself was reassuring. To the people, the captain was a superior being, whether they liked him or not, a man from a different world: he knew what was happening, he had talked to Nelson; and if he remained as elegant and unperturbed as usual and calmly spoke of a glorious victory, then a glorious victory it would be. The small processions moved along each gun deck; down to the cockpit at the after end of the orlop, where the surgeons had stropped their knives and their assistants the loblolly boys had dragged out the midshipmen's mess table, ready for the amputations, and spread out sails to lay the wounded on: down further still to the dim secluded world of the magazines, where gunners' mates stood waiting all alone in the light of a candle flickering through an air-tight window, cut off from everyone else by wet blankets hanging over the entrances, and by the stringent rules which kept unauthorized people away from the powder.

There was talk of glory, and much more talk of the pleasures of going home. And there was also another thought in every-body's mind: prize-money. Pure avarice, it must be admitted, was a very strong motive for battle. The thirty-three enemy ships down there on the eastern horizon were thirty-three potential fortunes for the British captains. To go home and retire was what they unanimously wanted: to do it with a comfortable sum, enough to live on, was even more attractive. Thirty-three pos-sible prizes, and twenty-seven ships to share them: that was a race no captain wanted to be left behind in: if nothing else had made them crowd on sail, that would have done so. Captain Digby of the Africa, who had lost the fleet in the night, was coming gallantly down from the northward all alone under every sail; and he was a man who knew what he was doing for he had collected £60,000 in prize-money by the time he was 30. It was a very much smaller incentive to lower ranks: for every thousand pounds of a captain's share of a prize, a seaman's share was slightly under two pounds. But still, that was something – it was more than a month's pay – and while seamen grumbled at the unfairness of it, they counted the chances and spent the money in imagination.

The French and Spanish captains also made their rounds. Lucas of the *Redoutable* marched round his decks preceded by men with fifes and drums. His crew, imbued with their training in small-arms fighting, shouted to remind him he had promised to let them board an enemy. In the *Bucentaure*, the Imperial Eagle entrusted by the Emperor to the fleet was paraded round the decks, carried by two cadets and followed by Villeneuve and his staff, the captain of the ship, Magendie, and General Contamine, who commanded the French troops who were embarked. Everywhere there were shouts of 'Vive l'Empereur!

Vive l'amiral!' And the Eagle with its youthful guard was stationed at the foot of the mainmast for the battle.

By such means, a fighting spirit was aroused in the Frenchmen. Among the seamen it was sincere enough. No doubt they had often been told of their own shortcomings, but a time always comes, in any fleet or army, when criticism has to change to praise. Now, they were reminded of the Emperor's expectation and persuaded they were a match for anyone: men manning guns felt satisfied with their own rate of fire, and did not know, or did not believe, that Englishmen doing the same could do it twice as fast. Some of them, in what seemed the impregnable strength of their ships, are said to have felt sorry for the English bearing down on them. But their senior officers knew what was likely to happen, and when they encouraged their men with talk of victory, it was hollow and insincere.

The Spaniards in general were closer to despair. It was not their battle. Centuries of war at sea had left a tradition among them that the English were murderous robbers. But in the last two months the French had seemed as hateful. They had no wish or reason to fight for Napoleon's glory: 'Vive l'Empereur!' meant less than nothing to them. There were brave men among them, ready to do their best; but, unlike the French, they knew they were inefficient. Their decks were cluttered with miserable landsmen and soldiers, two days at sea and still as sick as dogs. Their only comfort was in God: their navy was more pious in its observances than either the English or the French. While the French paraded their Eagle, the Spaniards hoisted crosses in their mizzen rigging, and in at least one ship, the *San Juan Nepocumeno*, the captain assembled the whole of his crew for prayers and absolution.

This was the captain who had said the fleet was doomed, and although at that moment he was unjust to Villeneuve, he merits sympathy. His name was Don Cosme Churruca: a handsome, melancholy, learned man of 45, well known in Spain as a scientific navigator – a model of the Spanish officers who followed a high tradition but now were given intolerable crews.

'If you hear my ship has been captured,' he wrote before the battle, 'you will know I am dead.' It was said that the government owed him nine years' pay, so that he had to command his ship in clothes that were almost threadbare; and also that he was recently married, and had broken short his honeymoon to put to sea. Those were troubles of his own, but others he shared with all the Spanish captains: mistrusting his admiral and despising his crew, he was fated to fight a battle he knew was hopeless, for a cause he did not believe in.

When his chaplain had administered the Sacrament to all hands, Churruca made a speech to them which represented the last resort of naval command. 'In God's name,' he was quoted as saying, 'I promise eternal blessedness to all who do their duty.' Those who did not, he added, would instantly be shot or, if they happened to escape his eyes and the eyes of his gallant officers, they would live the rest of their lives in wretchedness. A reward in heaven, summary execution, or misery on earth: this was all that was offered to the Spanish sailors.

Eleven o'clock: the Victory about three miles from the enemy line, and the Royal Sovereign a little closer. Individual ships could be identified, and from both sides people could plainly see how the battle was going to open.

The French and Spanish ships were still manoeuvring to form their line of battle. Most of them were in their proper order, or near it, but the line was still irregular – and so it remained. Altogether, a dozen ships had fallen to leeward of the rest, some through inferior handling and some to avoid running down the ships ahead of them; they failed in all their attempts to haul up again to their stations, perhaps because their wind was cut off by the ships that were in the line. There were gaps in the line where they should have been, and so many parts of the line were doubled that the British thought it must be deliberate, although it was useless as a tactical formation. The worst of the gaps was immediately astern of the *Bucentaure*, where three ships were missing. The leading squadron was close-hauled, but the rear of the fleet was steering a point farther off the wind, and the whole line had formed a curve with its concave side towards the British fleet.

Nelson was steering for the twelfth ship in the line, which by chance – he did not know it yet – was the *Bucentaure*. The eleventh ship, the next ahead of her, was more conspicuous and sooner recognized: the gigantic *Santisima Trinidad*, the largest ship in the world. Nelson had fought her before at the Battle of Cape St. Vincent and knew her well. His own division was following him as closely as it could. Astern of the Victory, the Temeraire and Captain Fremantle's Neptune, both three-deckers of ninety-eight guns, were so close that they had to haul out of her wake, the Temeraire to starboard and the Neptune to port. Also to port and astern were the Euryalus and the three other frigates, waiting for the captains to come back from the flagship, the small cutter Entreprenante and the schooner Pickle: her four small guns were manned and ready, and looked, as someone remarked long afterwards, about as dangerous as two pairs of Wellington boots. Astern again came the Leviathan and Conqueror; and then at longer intervals Britannia and Ajax, Sir Edward Berry in the Agamemnon and Captain Codrington in the Orion. Far behind were the Minotaur and Spartiate, living up to her reputation of sailing slowly in daylight.

On the poop of the Victory, Nelson was surrounded by devoted friends who knew him very well: Hardy, the captain of the ship; Pasco, the flag lieutenant; Dr. Beatty the surgeon; Mr. Scott the admiral's secretary, and Dr. Scott the chaplain, who was also his secretary for foreign affairs; Blackwood of the Euryalus and the captains of the other frigates, one of whom had been his flag lieutenant at the Battle of the Nile. All of these men, all through the morning, were worried about Nelson's personal safety. Again and again, they discussed it together, out of his hearing, but none of them dared to tell him directly, like Napoleon's generals at Waterloo, that his life was of special value and should not be unduly risked.

Blackwood was the first who tried to do something about it.

He suggested Nelson should move his flag to the Euryalus. There was some logic in a commander-in-chief directing affairs from a frigate, which could keep out of the heat of the battle and out of the smoke. But Nelson only said it would set a bad example.

Dr. Beatty took Dr. Scott aside to say he was afraid his Lordship would be a target for enemy marksmen: he wished he would cover the stars on his coat. Both the Scotts said the admiral would be displeased with anyone who suggested such a thing, but Beatty felt so strongly about it that he said he would risk it: he would tell the admiral when he gave him the sick report for the day. 'Take care, Doctor, what you are about,' the secretary said, 'I would not be the man to mention such a matter to him.' Beatty hovered respectfully on the edge of the group that surrounded Nelson, waiting for his chance. But it never came. Nelson was busy with the captains of the frigates until the last moment, when he ordered everyone to go to their battle quarters, and Beatty, still worrying, had to go down to the orlop.

Blackwood thought of something else: the Victory, he pointed out, would be singled out by the enemy because she was the flagship: would it not be proper to let one or two other ships go ahead of her, to draw off the enemy's attention? This was a more subtle suggestion, invoking the safety of the ship and her crew, not only of the admiral. Nelson agreed. He signalled the Temeraire to pass the Victory. She crept up even closer to the Victory's starboard quarter, but very slowly. Blackwood went to Hardy: would he point out to the admiral that the Temeraire would not be able to take her station ahead unless the Victory shortened sail? But Hardy was certain Nelson would not hear of that: he had been fretting all morning about the slowness of the advance to battle. And shortly after, Nelson changed his mind: leaning over the taffrail, he hailed the Temeraire: 'I'll thank you, Captain Harvey, to take your proper station, which is astern of the Victory.'

All their attempts had failed.

*

Collingwood in the Royal Sovereign was facing identical dangers – even more perhaps, for his ship being newly coppered was drawing ahead of his division, and sailing full tilt at the enemy unsupported. He was never a man to show his feelings, as Nelson so plainly did. Nobody could have known what he thought of the danger. The only glimpse of him anyone recorded, in that final hour, was from a midshipman who said the thought of glory had made the old admiral feel quite young again. Nor was he a man to have loving friends to worry about him. Having changed ships there were only two men on board who knew him well – the two lieutenants he had brought with him. One of them suggested he ought not to wear a cocked hat, which made him conspicuous; but he answered testily that he had never fought in anything else and did not propose to begin.

The Tonnant, next astern of him, was lagging: the Mars and Belleisle, third and fourth in line, had had to shorten sail to stay astern of her. Collingwood signalled them to change places. Both reset their studding sails. As the Belleisle drew ahead, the Tonnant's band was playing a popular tune called 'Britons strike home', and the captains hailed each other: 'A glorious day for old England! We shall have one apiece before night!'

Collingwood was steering for the sixteenth ship from the enemy's rear. That was taking on more opponents than Nelson had ordered, but he may have made his choice because he recognized her as the flagship of the Spanish Vice-Admiral de Alava – the black-painted *Santa Ana*, 112 guns, another of the huge Spanish ships. There was a difference between his approach and Nelson's. Nelson's division was sailing square to the enemy, but Collingwood's was at an angle – partly because his own line was somewhat to starboard of his wake, and partly because of the curve in the enemy line. So, in the final hour of the approach, his ships began to pick their own opponents and alter course towards them. Belleisle, Mars and Tonnant continued to follow him. Captain Cooke in the Bellerophon bore off to starboard and steered for the Spanish *Bahama*, five ships astern of the *Santa Ana*. The Achille and Colossus followed his lead.

Revenge, the next in line, chose the Spanish *San Ildefonso*, sixth ship from the enemy's rear. Astern of her came Defiance, Dreadnought, Thunderer, Defence, Polyphemus and Swiftsure. Last of all, the Prince, still sailing like a haystack, had strayed across to the rear of Nelson's line.

As the moment approached, the tension grew almost unbearable: the waiting had been so long. Men suddenly remembered something quite mundane: they were hungry, and the battle was going to start exactly at dinner-time. Some captains had foreseen it and ordered the cooks to have the beef and biscuit ready an hour early: others less wise ordered cheese up from the holds, and a half ration of rum. Officers, whose cabins had been dismantled, ate where they stood, or grouped round the rudder head, which they used as a table. Some captains called their junior lieutenants up from the gun decks for a final word – mostly to tell them to hold their fire. Captain Hargood of the Belleisle pointed out the black bulk of the *Santa Ana*: 'Gentlemen, I have only to say that I shall pass close under the stern of that ship. Put in two round shot and then a grape, and give her *that*.'

And Nelson also felt the tension, and the need for a final word. He said to Blackwood, who had been his most constant companion all the morning, 'I will now amuse the fleet with a signal. Do you not think there is one yet wanting?' Blackwood said everyone seemed to know exactly what to do. Nelson thought for a moment, and then said, 'Suppose we telegraph "Nelson confides that every man will do his duty".' Somebody suggested 'England' instead of 'Nelson', and Nelson accepted the change with pleasure. With an air of boyish gaiety, he called the flag lieutenant: 'Mr. Pasco, I wish to say to the fleet "England confides that every man will do his duty." You must be quick, for I have one more to make, which is for close action.' Pasco asked to be allowed to use 'expects' instead of 'confides' because 'expects' was in Popham's signal book, but 'confides' would have to be spelt. 'That will do, Pasco, make it directly,'

Nelson said. And at 11.35 the most famous battle signal ever made was hoisted to the yards and mastheads of the Victory.

'England expects that every man will do his duty': the phrase inspired generations of Englishmen. Yet it was not received with unanimous joy in the fleet. Ships cheered it, but in some of them the cheer itself had a dutiful ring about it. Collingwood, seeing the flags, said: 'I wish Nelson would stop signalling. We know well enough what to do' – but when the whole signal was read to him, he approved it cordially enough. In the Euryalus, nobody bothered to repeat it to the crew; and in the Ajax, the officer who was sent to read it out on the gun decks heard sailors muttering 'Do my duty? I've always done my duty, haven't you, Jack?'

Nelson's first instinct had been right, as it always was in matters of that kind. 'England' was too impersonal; 'expects' was too mandatory. Nelson's confidence would have meant much more to the fleet than England's expectation. 'Nelson confides' – they would have cheered that all right; that was what they would have liked to hear. England was far away: England was not the navy, and this was a naval occasion. But Nelson was there, he was with them, one of them: he was their pride.

When the flags were hauled down, his last signal was hoisted: 'Engage the enemy more closely.' It flew at the masthead until it was shot away.

'Now I can do no more,' he said to Blackwood. 'We must trust to the great disposer of all events, and to the justice of our cause.' A few minutes later, he gave the frigate captains their final instructions and sent them back to their ships. 'God bless you, Blackwood,' he said. 'I shall not speak to you again.'

Ten minutes to noon: a burst of smoke was seen from the French Fougueux, and the sound of her guns came rolling across the sea.

The Fougueux, next astern of the Santa Ana, had fired a full broadside at the Royal Sovereign at a range of a thousand yards. A few seconds later, other French and Spanish ships near the rear of the line opened fire at the Royal Sovereign, Belleisle, Mars and Tonnant, and the whole of the allied fleet ran up its national flags. One of those first broadsides killed two of the Tonnant's bandsmen, still playing on the poop. At noon the Royal Sovereign fired the first British guns, but only to cover herself with smoke which drifted down wind ahead of her. From every ship in the fleet men watched her in fascination, standing on defenceless, with all her sails still set, into the fire of half a dozen enemies, unable yet to bring her own guns to bear.

Collingwood ordered the crew to lie down: so did Captain Hargood of the Belleisle, three minutes astern of him. Hargood climbed on to the carriage of a gun, the better to see the enemy ships ahead, already half covered by their smoke. For a few minutes, people remembered, there was an awful silence. In the Belleisle, it was only broken by Hargood's orders, and the voice of the master repeating them: 'Steady – starboard a little – steady so.' But again the flashes from the enemy fleet, the smoke and the rumble of the guns. The fire began to tell. The mizzen topmast was shot away and fell in a tangle of rigging: the ensign was cut down and hastily rehoisted: a crash when a round shot split the hull, and the whirring sound of splinters: a sudden scream of pain. Paul Nicolas, the officer of Marines, 16 years old, saw and heard it all too clearly, standing on the forward edge of the poop, stricken with horror at the sight of a man blown to pieces. Almost everyone was lying down: he desperately wanted to lie down, but the captain was standing and his own commander, the lieutenant of Marines, was pacing up and down the poop, looking calm and composed. He joined him, and tried to look the same. In ten minutes a score of men were wounded and carried down to the surgeon: a dozen dead lay on the decks. 'Shall we not show our broadside and fire?' the first lieutenant dared to ask. 'No,' Hargood said, 'we are ordered to go through the line, and go through she shall, by God!'

In the last few hundred yards, the Royal Sovereign's studding sails were all shot away and fell trailing in the water, and her speed began to slacken.

The captains of the *Santa Ana* and *Fougueux* both saw that she was steering to pass between them: the *Santa Ana* backed her mizzen topsail to check her own way, and the *Fougueux* set more sail to close her. Nelson, watching from the Victory, exclaimed in admiration: 'See how that noble fellow Collingwood carries his ship into action!' Pasco, with his glass to his eye, said: 'There is a topgallant yard gone!' 'Whose?' Nelson asked. 'Is it the Royal Sovereign's?' Pasco said no. 'Collingwood is doing well,' Nelson said. At the same time, Collingwood was saying to his captain, 'What would Nelson give to be here!' – conscious of the honour of being first into battle. He told the captain to steer for the bowsprit of the *Fougueux* and carry it away. But the *Fougueux*, seeing his intention, bore away to avoid him. The Royal Sovereign passed close under the unprotected stern of the *Santa Ana*, and as she went she fired the fifty guns of her port broadside, double-shotted, at a range of thirty yards, and then within a minute fired half of them again – a hundred and twenty-five round shot. Putting her helm hard to starboard she ranged up the lee side of the *Santa Ana*, so close that the yards of the two ships locked together; and, to the watchers in the fleet, both ships disappeared in the cloud of their own gunsmoke.

By then the Victory's ordeal had begun. At the same range, a thousand yards, the *Héros*, *Bucentaure* and *Santisima Trinidad* opened fire on her, at first only using single guns to test the range. Very soon after, the five ships of the enemy's van began to do the same, although they were too far away for any effective fire. The single shots continued, until one of them tore a hole in the Victory's main topgallant sail. The French saw the hole, raised a cheer and started to fire their broadsides. Almost at once, a cannon-ball killed Mr. Scott the secretary, standing talking to Hardy on the poop. Marines threw the mangled body overboard, but Nelson saw it: 'Is that poor Scott who is gone? Poor fellow!' And another killed eight of the Marines, who were drawn up on the poop. Nelson told their captain to disperse the survivors round the ship.

It seemed to the Victory's officers, surveying the scene with calm professional interest, that the enemy were aiming high to bring down her masts and disable her before she could close with them. But the French were doing nothing so subtle, until the very last few hundred yards. The rolling of their ships in the swell was making their gunfire wild, especially in elevation, as Nelson had undoubtedly foreseen. The ships of the van gave it up, and turned their attention to the Africa, coming down from the northward all alone. Villeneuve and his captain, Magendie, saw that the gunnery was far less accurate than it should have been. And Lucas, astern of him in the *Redoutable*, indulged his habit of pointing out other men's mistakes: he called most of his captains of guns up to the quarter-deck, showed them that the other ships were wasting shot, and told them to hold their fire until it was certain, and only then to aim to dismast the Victory.

From the sheer quantity of shot, the Victory suffered. Like the Belleisle, her mizzen topmast fell, and all her studding sails were shot away. A ball ploughed across the quarter-deck and cut the tiller ropes and broke the wheel: forty men were assembled below to man the tiller, and steering orders were sent or shouted down to them. Twenty men were killed and thirty wounded before she could fire a shot. Nelson and Hardy walked the quarter-deck in conversation: a shot struck the deck ahead of them and passed between them, and a splinter of wood from it tore off the buckle of Hardy's shoe. They both stopped, and people saw them look at each other, each thinking the other was wounded. Then Nelson smiled and said: 'This is too warm work, Hardy, to last long.' And he added that in all his battles he had never seen more cool courage than the Victory's crew was showing.

The attack developed in just the same way as the Royal Sovereign's. All the French and Spanish in the centre could see that the Victory meant to cut through the line either ahead or astern of the *Bucentaure*. Ahead, the *Bucentaure* was close to the *Santisima Trinidad*; astern, there was still a gap left by ships that had fallen to leeward. Lucas, a boastful man but an excellent seaman, made sail to close it, and succeeded in getting so close that officers on the admiral's poop shouted in alarm or annoyance to him that he was going to run them down. By his account, his bowsprit lightly touched the stern rail of the *Bucentaure*.

Hardy watched the manoeuvre. It left him no gap to go through. It seemed impossible, he said to Nelson, to pass through the enemy's line without going on board one of their ships. 'I cannot help it,' Nelson said. 'It does not signify which one we run on board of. Go on board which you please. Take your choice.' Hardy sent the master below to the tiller flat to order the helm to port, and the ship slowly swung towards the *Redoutable*. As she swung, the *Bucentaure* fired a final scattered broadside. Unlike the *Fougueux*, Lucas did not give way. The Victory crashed into the bows of the *Redoutable*: Lucas's men flung grappling-irons on board her. She passed so close to the *Bucentaure* that their rigging touched, and with a puff of wind men could have reached out and seized hold of the French ensign. As her forecastle passed the *Bucentaure*'s ornate and beautiful stern she fired her port carronade, the largest of guns in the fleet, loaded with a 68-pound ball and a keg of five hundred musket-balls, and then the whole of her port broadside at point-blank range of the windows of Villeneuve's cabin, smashing the stern to pieces and spreading ghastly havoc along the decks. The dust of shattered woodwork floated across her.

In the era of gunpowder, smoke was a factor which influenced every battle, and in the feeble breeze of the day of Trafalgar it shrouded everything. Sometimes an eddy cleared it for a moment, and sometimes in lulls in the firing it drifted away and suddenly revealed the whole of the panorama of the battle. But whenever the firing was heavy, friends and enemies were hidden by banks of it. Ships loomed through it unexpectedly at the range of a pistol-shot: beyond them, only topmasts could be seen.

And the feebleness of the breeze was the cause of another distinctive feature of Trafalgar: its slowness. In the approach, with all sail set and the wind astern, the ships had been slow enough; but probably, once the battle was joined, not one of them moved at more than one mile an hour, and to turn them, to alter course or bring their guns to bear, took many minutes. As they tacked and wore, manoeuvring for position, it was like a macabre dance, but infinitely slow: or like a fight to the death of prehistoric monsters, cumbersome and huge.

The smoke and the slowness, combined with the intense excitement of it, upset people's sense of time and cut them off from each other, so that many of them believed their ship was all alone, perhaps for hours, surrounded by enemies, without a friend to help them. But no ship was. The entire battle was fought in an area a mile and a half long and half a mile across, and within it, including the frigates, there were approximately

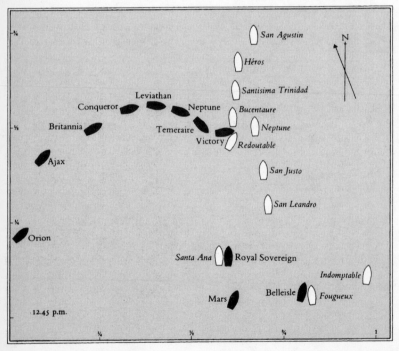

12.45 Victory cuts the line

sixty ships. One's friends might be busily engaged, but they were not far away.

It was so in the Royal Sovereign. Locked together with the *Santa Ana*, blazing away at a range of two or three yards and engaging other ships with her starboard broadside, she seemed to her crew to be alone for hours. Even Collingwood believed it was twenty minutes. But in fact the Belleisle came through the same gap in the line three minutes after her, and fired her own broadside into the *Santa Ana*'s stern, loaded as Hargood had ordered with two round shot and a grape shot on top of them. And the Royal Sovereign's men, for the most part, in the din and horror of their own engagement, were unaware of that fearsome blast of shot.

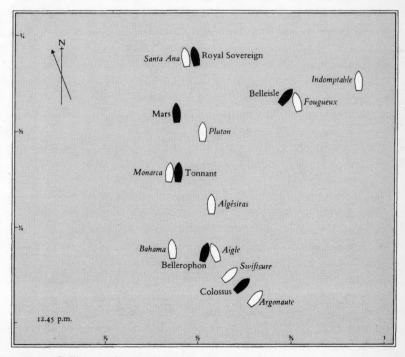

12.45 Collingwood's squadron

The Belleisle stood on through the line, firing her other broadside at a ship astern of the *Santa Ana*. Beyond the line, Hargood sighted the *Indomptable*, one of those that had fallen to leeward. 'There's your ship, sir,' he said to his master, 'place me close alongside of her.' She altered course and crept on, but ever more slowly because her yards and sails and rigging were already hanging in confusion overhead. Before she went far, the *Fougueux* came out of the smoke, close on her starboard beam, and rammed her amidships. The bowsprit and fore yardarm of the *Fougueux* came crashing in over the gangway, ground aft along the quarter-deck and tangled in the rigging; and two more ships were fastened together in combat.

Nobody left a deliberate first-hand account of the scenes on the gun decks in these close encounters. If one puts together the scraps that are known, they make a picture like a medieval hell. It was a hell of noise: cannon thundering, crashing back in recoil and flashing fire: the shouts and yells, occasionally cheers, of hundreds of men as they loaded, rammed, hauled on the tackles or hove the carriages round with handspikes; the awful rending crashes as enemy shot smashed through the sides and splintered the timber; and the screams of the wounded.

It was a hell of vision too. You could not see far, the narrow space was full of blinding smoke: within your sight, the dim square light of the nearest gunports, slow-matches burning in their tubs, the gush of flames from the touchholes which scorched the beams above, men staggering towards the hatches clutching their wounds, the surgeon's assistants heaving up the wounded who could not walk, men shoving their dead and dying companions through the ports and overboard into the sea: the powder-monkeys, small boys running through the horrors carrying cartridges; and the blood, which flowed from side to side as the ship rolled, and made curious patterns on the deck.

All this was compounded when ships were locked together. The enemy's hull cut off the light from one of the rows of ports, and made the scene even darker. Sometimes, at point-blank range, the red-hot blast of a gun came straight through a port and scorched everything and everyone inside it. And where the hulls were touching, the guns could not be run out, but had to be fired with their muzzles inside the ports, so that all their smoke came back on the deck and the concussion deafened men for life.

These scenes were far worse in the French and Spanish ships than in the British, because the British could fire their guns so much more quickly. The first broadside of the Victory disabled two hundred men in the *Bucentaure* and smashed or dismounted twenty of her guns: before she passed, the Victory was ready to begin to fire again, but the *Bucentaure*, or any French or Spanish ship, took two or three times as long.*

The upper decks had less of this hellish quality. Their dangers were different. In close combat there was less risk up there from cannon fire: the guns of both ships might blaze away, but most of them were down below, and the fire of other enemy ships was restricted for fear of hitting their friend. But upper-deck men stood there, face to face with the enemy, perhaps a hundred of them plainly in sight and not ten yards away. Some of them had muskets, swivel guns and the smaller cannon, 12-pounders, which could blast the deck with grape shot. But most of them were not there to fight, unless they had to: they were there to work the ship, to make or shorten sail, to tack or wear. They did not carry arms, which would have hindered them, especially in the rigging. If they were called on to board, or to repel boarders, they snatched up weapons stowed round the feet of the masts. But otherwise, they went on with their jobs and let the enemy go on with theirs.

The design of the ships kept the enemy at a certain distance. Their greatest width was just above the waterline, and higher up

---

* There are different reports of the precise length of time it took to reload and fire the guns. No doubt it varied, from one gun's crew to another, and from one deck to another: the 32-pounders on the lower decks took longer than the 24- and 12-pounders. A broadside did not mean that all the guns were fired exactly simultaneously; and after the first broadside, given a target, each gun was fired as soon as it was ready. What mattered was that the British could fire much more quickly than anyone else, and with better aim.

their topsides had the inward curve which designers still call a 'tumblehome'. So even when the sides of two ships were grinding together, there was usually a space of fifteen or twenty feet between their upper decks, too wide to be easily crossed. As for the muskets, they were very inaccurate: it needed more luck than skill to hit a man half a ship's length away, or even across the width of a rolling deck. Musketmen spoke of annoying the enemy with their fire.

In some of the close encounters at Trafalgar, furious fights flared up among the upper-deck men. But in others, men went about their business, taking what cover they could from casual snipers. And whatever happened, the senior officers stood on the quarter-decks, taking care to look as if they scorned the danger. At the height of the battle against the *Santa Ana*, Collingwood gave an example of real disdain. Well known for his exaggerated care of naval property, he saw a studding sail still hanging over the starboard bulwarks. 'Come and help me take that in,' he said to his first lieutenant. 'We shall want it again some other day.' And under the eyes of the *Santa Ana*'s crew, the two of them went and folded the sail, and stowed it in one of the boats.

The British had strong feelings against the deliberate killing of individual men, and never began it. Some of the French stationed musketeers in the tops, fifty feet up their masts, to try to pick off men on the decks below; but Nelson would not allow it because, he said, there was too much danger of setting sails on fire. And apart from that specific reason, there was a general feeling that small-arms fighting was unworthy of a navy, even perhaps unsporting. In the navy, you fought the enemy ships, not the men in them: you fought to capture them, as nearly intact as they could be – and ships were not captured, much less were battles won, by shooting individual seamen. The great gun was the proper naval weapon. Men must get hurt, but that was a different matter: everyone took his chance.

The *Fougueux* and Belleisle wrecked each other. When at last they drifted apart, both believed they had been fighting all alone, and both had lost all count of time. 'We found ourselves entirely surrounded by enemies,' wrote an officer of the *Fougueux*. 'We were lying in this dismasted state,' wrote one of the Belleisle, 'surrounded by enemy's ships, and not having seen the colours of a friendly ship for the previous two hours.' Both were mistaken. But both ships were in the predicament of being unable to move in the very centre of the battle. The *Fougueux* had lost her main- and mizzen-masts, and the Belleisle lost all three. Falling over the side, the sails and rigging covered most of her gunports and only a few of her guns could still be fired. Two lieutenants were killed, and Captain Hargood was knocked down by a splinter which bruised him from his neck to his hip. French ships came up ahead and astern of her, and fired from bearings where she could not reply. But nobody despaired. They fastened a pike to the stump of the mainmast and hoisted a flag on that, and carried on. They moved guns and ran them out of the sternports, and tried to turn the ship by putting oars out of the gunroom ports and rowing her round. In this situation, Captain Hargood encountered the captain of Marines, whose name was John Owen, and offered him a bunch of grapes; and they stood on the quarter-deck eating the grapes, and told each other the ship was doing nobly.

Astern of them in the smoke, three hundred yards away, the Mars and Tonnant were in battle. The Mars was one ship that failed to cut through the line. She met a French ship, the *Pluton*, bow to bow, and hauled to the wind to bring her guns to bear. The two of them fought it out for twenty minutes or so, when the Mars had to come up closer to the wind to avoid falling on board the *Santa Ana*. That was a perilous and perhaps a mistaken move. It exposed her stern to the *Pluton*. And it happened just as the *Fougueux* drew away from her clash with the Belleisle. The *Fougueux*, undaunted, caught a glimpse of the Mars and gave her a broadside. So did the *Pluton*. Between them, they cut her rigging to pieces and blew off the head of the captain, George Duff, whose young son was on board with him as a midshipman.

She drifted away, unmanageable, with ninety-eight men killed and wounded. Her masts were all standing, but nothing was supporting them: every one of the shrouds and braces had been shot away. No sail could be set, and her officers could not bring her to battle again. Her crew spent the rest of the day, and several succeeding days, in knotting and splicing the rigging together to save the masts.

The Tonnant used different tactics. She fought and quickly defeated a Spanish ship. The Spaniard struck his colours, but she was too busy to take possession of the prize, because she was also engaged with the *Algésiras*, the flagship of Villeneuve's hot-headed critic Admiral Magon. As he approached, Magon fired into the Tonnant's stern and split her rudder. Captain Tyler of the Tonnant – whether he intended it or could not help it – swung his ship across the path of Magon's, and Magon rammed him amidships and drove his bowsprit up over the deck and into the mainmast rigging. There it stuck, and the ships came to rest with the Tonnant lying across the bow of the *Algésiras*.

It was a good position for the Tonnant: she could fire the whole of her starboard broadside, and the *Algésiras* could only reply with a few of her forward guns. It was also a good position for boarding. There was no gap, and men could climb through the rigging. Here a murderous upper-deck battle developed. Magon had musketmen in the tops, firing down on the Tonnant below them. Captain Tyler was shot in the thigh and carried below, abruptly leaving command to his first lieutenant. Several lieutenants had a hurried conference. It was interrupted by shouts of 'A l'abordage!' A mass of Frenchmen, most of the crew it seemed, came swarming over their bows. The Tonnant's Marines engaged them with musketry, and the forecastle men turned their guns which were loaded with grape and mowed them down. Only one of the French reached the Tonnant's deck: somebody pinned him through the calf of his leg with a pike and others were about to cut him down, but an officer saved him and sent him down to the surgeon.

Everything was in the Tonnant's favour: the advantage of position, superior gunnery, and most of all the absolute unquestioning confidence that any British ship could beat a French one. The upper decks of both the ships were swept almost clear of men by grape and musketry. In the *Algésiras*, the upper gun deck was desolated too, and its survivors made their way to the lower deck and took the places of men who had fallen there. Nobody could have doubted Magon's courage. Confronted at last by the battle he had wanted, he saw his ship wrecked and his men beginning to fail: he was shot in the arm and a splinter wounded his thigh, and he still stood on his quarter-deck directing the crew. But other French officers began, as it were, to look over their shoulders, hoping for help from another ship in their fleet, and there was none in sight. While that fatal doubt began, a sailor from the Tonnant called Fitzgerald showed the superfluity of daring that carried the British through. He boarded the *Algésiras* all alone, ran up her rigging to the topmast, cut down the French flag and wrapped it round his waist, and then came down again – but before he reached the deck he was shot, and he fell in the sea between the ships and was never seen again.

The end of this dire encounter came when all three masts of the *Algésiras* fell, shot through below the deck. A lieutenant and sixty men of the Tonnant jumped over her bows and took possession. At the foot of the poop ladder, they found Admiral Magon, lying dead.

A mile north of the Tonnant and Royal Sovereign, Nelson was fighting the other separate battle he had planned, and the Victory was aboard of the *Redoutable*, Captain Lucas.

When the Victory rammed the port bow of the *Redoubtable*, she carried it round to the eastward and the sides of the two ships came together. And men on the Victory were astonished to see that the *Redoutable* slammed shut her gunports.

That shut off her main armament, and it was the last thing any British ship would have done. But it was part of the drill that

Lucas had taught his crew. Unable to train them in gunnery, he had become obsessed, far more than other captains, with the merits of hand-to-hand small-arms fighting. To board the enemy: that was the aim of his personal tactics, the vision of glory he had put before his men. And to have fallen alongside Nelson's flagship offered a chance of glory higher than he had dreamed.

A ship could be boarded from deck to deck, or through the rigging or through the gunports. He had no intention of letting himself be boarded through his gunports, so he shut them: he meant to fight his battle on the upper deck and aloft, where he was strongest. Up there, he had a hundred men with muskets and bayonets, a large number also with cutlasses and pistols, and others specially trained in throwing hand-grenades. His tops were crowded with musketeers and grenadiers, and his gun decks were more than half empty. It was the kind of fighting the British despised, the kind they believed could never capture a ship. But Lucas had convinced himself it could. As the two ships touched, his musketeers opened rapid fire, which might have been two hundred shots a minute, and his grenadiers threw several hundred hand-grenades on board.

If Nelson's friends could have foreseen that chance would bring them alongside the ship of a man with such ideas, their anxiety for his safety would have become despair. After close action had been joined, his work was done, and so was Hardy's, until the outcome of the immediate battle could be seen. And therefore they did what they always did at sea when they had no pressing business: they paced up and down the quarter-deck together, from the break of the poop to the hatch and back again. Of course they could see the musketeers: some of them were only forty feet away. And they could see their own people falling round them, hit by the unprecedented fire. But it was unthinkable that a commander-in-chief or a captain should take cover, or vary his routine in deference to the enemy. The code of conduct compelled them to take no notice, and indeed they may have been so absorbed in the progress of great events that they were hardly thinking of the danger.

The fight had been in progress twenty minutes when Nelson was shot, by a musketeer from the mizzen top which was fifty feet above him. He had just turned at the hatchway and was facing aft, and the ball, coming downward, struck him on the left shoulder and entered his chest. Hardy walked on a few paces unaware. When he turned, two seamen and the sergeant-major of Marines were lifting Nelson, who had fallen in the blood of Scott the secretary. 'They have done for me at last, Hardy,' Nelson said. Hardy said he hoped not. 'Yes,' Nelson said, 'my backbone is shot through.' The seamen carried him down to Dr. Beatty in the cockpit.

So fierce and successful was Lucas's fire that five minutes after Nelson was shot, the Victory's upper deck was almost empty of men. About fifty were wounded, and most of the rest had taken cover somewhere. The firing slackened, perhaps through lack of targets. And as the great guns of the *Redoutable* had not been fired at all since the ships had touched, Hardy thought she had struck, or was ready to strike. He ordered the Victory's starboard guns to cease fire.

But Lucas had not struck: on the contrary, he was sure he was winning, and when the Victory's guns fell silent it convinced him. He had a bugle sounded, which was his signal to board, and he ordered his mainsail yard cut down so that it would fall across the gap and form a bridge. His cutlass and pistol men ran up from below, and ahead of them a cadet named Yul and four seamen scrambled across the Victory's anchor and reached her deck. For a moment of glory, Lucas believed he was capturing the flagship, and he claimed ever after that he would have done so: but at that moment the Temeraire came out of the smoke and ran aboard him on the other side.

It seems unlikely that his method could ever have succeeded. He had killed a good many upper-deck men, but below deck the Victory was very much alive, and her fifty starboard guns had been methodically smashing his ship to pieces under his feet, the 32-pounders firing right through her, in at one side and out at the other. When the guns were run out, their muzzles touched her sides, and the blast of them set her splintered timber on fire. For fear that a fire would spread to the Victory, a man was put at each gun with a bucket of water, which he threw into the hole the shot had made. After the pause that Hardy ordered, she started again, and when the Temeraire hove in sight the Victory's gunners were told to load with three round shot and a smaller charge of powder, and to depress their guns so that if their shot went through the *Redoutable* they would go through her bottom and would not hit the Temeraire beyond her. No ship could have stood that treatment very long.

Lucas supposed that the Temeraire had seen that the Victory was beaten and had come aboard him on purpose to rescue her. But in fact, Captain Harvey of the Temeraire could not see anything at all. His ship had been in action with six enemies as she followed the Victory through the line, and was badly damaged in the rigging; and then she had run into such a bank of smoke that Harvey lost sight of the Victory, although she must have been within a hundred yards. He ordered his gunners to cease fire, in case they fired into her. When he found her again, he placed the Temeraire to give the *Redoutable* a raking broadside. But the two ships drifted down on him, and he could not avoid them.

Lucas's position then was hopeless – a two-decked ship with a three-decker fast on each side. But he still would not strike his colours. The extra height of the Temeraire brought her upper tier of guns to the level of Lucas's upper deck where the whole of his boarding-party was standing, and her broadside put over two hundred men out of action. He was wounded by it, but he stayed on deck. His ship, he said afterwards, was no more than a heap of debris. Above her orlop, there was hardly a man unhurt. Her main and foremasts fell, over the starboard side, across the Temeraire. And the Temeraire's topmasts fell the other way, across the poop and quarter-deck of the *Redoutable*, and bound the ships together with hundreds of ropes and spars.

And next the *Fougueux*, already crippled by her fight with the Belleisle, was seen in the smoke to leeward. The three ships drifted helplessly down on her, and the Temeraire fell aboard of her. It was a sight that old men said had never been seen before – four ships-of-the-line all aboard of each other, all more or less dismasted, all heading the same way, as close as if they had all been moored at a pier. The crew of the *Fougueux* had no more fight in them: after ten minutes she struck, and the Temeraire sent a few men on board to take possession. The *Redoutable* had also ceased to fire, but Lucas had not struck his colours. Only the Victory was in action. All the time, she had been firing her port guns at the *Bucentaure* and *Santisima Trinidad*, and she was still doing so.

The *Redoutable* was dead, a hulk; but still, for a while, she remained impregnable. The Victory had a prize-crew ready to take possession, but they could not cross the gap, and since she had shut her gunports they could not board her there. Neither side of her could be reached by a boat. Some seamen volunteered to jump overboard and swim under her bows and try to climb up there, but Hardy would not allow it. The problem was still unsolved when the Victory at last broke free, and set what sail she could, and brought her head up to the northward. Then she sent two midshipmen in a small boat, and they boarded the *Redoutable* unopposed. There were exactly three hundred dead men in her. Of her complement of six hundred and forty-three, only one hundred and twenty-one were unhurt: these for the most part were men whose work was below the waterline. Two hundred and twenty-two were in the hands of the surgeon, down on the orlop. The water in the hold below them was rising fast and threatened to drown them all, and four of the ship's six pumps were shot to pieces.

Yet still the fire had not gone out of Lucas. He would not surrender: he had to put it another way, as a demand and a threat. He hailed the Temeraire and requested them to send him some men to help him man the pumps – and if they refused, he said, he would set his ship on fire and burn the Temeraire, which could not escape from him. It was a gesture. The Temeraire got a boarding-party across. When a ship struck, it was usual to take the captain off, but they left Lucas where he was. They detested his method of fighting, but they admired his courage.

Down in the dimness of the Victory's cockpit, cut off from these scenes of action, was the scene of grief that Nelson's biographers have all described. Only five men were there, in the narrow pool of light that was thrown by a lantern. The thoughts of them all were distracted from the battle up above, just as the scene itself distracted attention afterwards from all the scenes of death and elation which surrounded it. Afterwards, they tried to remember everything that happened, and everything that Nelson said, and Dr. Beatty the surgeon wrote it down, giving the dying man a curiously formal turn of speech.

When Nelson was carried down there, several other wounded officers and about forty men were also brought down from the upper deck, and Beatty had just examined one of his closest friends and found that he was dead. Several of the wounded called to him: 'Mr. Beatty, Lord Nelson is here – Mr. Beatty, the Admiral is wounded.' He ran to help him, with Mr. Burke the purser, and took him from the seamen who had carried him below. They stumbled, Beatty remembered, but recovered themselves and put him in a midshipman's berth. Nelson asked who it was, and when he was told he said: 'Ah, Mr. Beatty, you can do nothing for me. I have but a short time to live: my back is shot through.'

Dr. Scott the devoted chaplain was giving lemonade to the wounded. He also came, wringing his hands in his grief and saying, 'Alas, Beatty, how prophetic you were!' They took off Nelson's clothes, with the help of Mr. Chevalier his steward and another of his personal servants, whose name was not recorded. 'Doctor, I told you so,' Nelson said to Scott. 'Doctor, I am gone.' And after a pause he added in a low voice: 'I have to leave Lady Hamilton, and my adopted daughter Horatia, as a legacy to my country.' But whether he said this to Scott, or whether Scott remembered it exactly, nobody can tell. Perhaps his mind had gone back to the morning, when he must have said some such thing to Blackwood and Hardy.

Beatty examined the wound and asked him his sensations, and he described them exactly: every minute he felt a gush of blood in his breast, he had no feeling in the lower part of his body, his breathing was difficult and it gave him a severe pain in the part of his spine where he had felt the bullet strike. Beatty convinced himself at once that he was dying. He sent a message to Hardy, but told nobody else except his two assistant surgeons.

Beatty came and went, to the amputations on the gunroom table and to the other wounded men who surrounded the little space that was cleared for Nelson. For he was not alone, or in any way secluded. Pasco the signal officer was lying wounded close enough to speak to him, and somebody rolled up the discarded bloodstained frock-coat with the stars sewn on it and put it under the head of a midshipman. Scott and Burke remained, with the two servants. They tried at first to make Nelson think he might recover, but he never had any doubt he was dying: 'It is nonsense, Mr. Burke, to suppose I can live. My sufferings are great, but they will all be soon over.' Beatty's description suggests that for an hour his mind was shocked and preoccupied with pain and a feeling of suffocation; but it cleared, and he began to think again about the battle, and later, when he knew his death was very close, about Lady Hamilton and Horatia.

The scene, so isolated and quiet in retrospect, took place in fact among a deafening noise – the cries of the wounded in the semi-darkness and the roar of the 32-pounders up above – and Scott and Burke were not always able to hear what Nelson said. Sometimes when the gunfire slackened the seamen above gave a cheer, and once when that happened Nelson asked the cause of it. Pasco raised himself up and told him another enemy ship had struck. Nelson grew more and more anxious to know what was happening, and repeatedly asked for Hardy. Beatty sent messages up to the deck, but Hardy could not come. 'Will no one bring Hardy to me? He must be killed: he is surely destroyed.' At length Hardy's aide-de-camp, a young midshipman named Richard Bulkeley, came down with a formal message: 'Circumstances respecting the fleet require Captain Hardy's presence on deck, but he will avail himself of the first favourable moment to visit his Lordship.' Nelson heard him give the message to Beatty, and asked who he was. 'It is Mr. Bulkeley, my Lord.' Some recollection came back to his mind. 'It is his voice,' he said; and then to the midshipman: 'Remember me to your father.'

Hardy had more than enough to do. While Nelson was out of action and Collingwood had not been informed, Hardy was not only captain of the ship but also the acting commander-in-chief: the fleet would still look to the Victory for signals. And the Victory herself was half crippled and heavily engaged. When she broke free of the *Redoutable*, his first concern was to have the wreckage cut away and to trim what sails remained, and get some steerage way on her. As she started to move, the tiller was hauled across to starboard – she was still being steered from the gun deck – and he brought her head up to the northward, intending no doubt to complete the manoeuvre Nelson had planned and Lucas had prevented: to pass up the lee side of the *Bucentaure* and engage her closely.

But by then it was hardly necessary: Villeneuve in his flagship had already been fought to a standstill by the methods the British excelled in – gunnery and ship-handling. When the Victory carried away the *Redoutable*, the long gap in the French and Spanish line, about a third of a mile, had been reopened astern of the *Bucentaure*, and the first four ships of Nelson's squadron had followed the Victory through it – the Temeraire, Neptune, Leviathan and Conqueror – and each of them, as she came slowly through, had raked the *Bucentaure* afresh with a terrible fire.

Villeneuve had been left by his fleet in the worst conceivable position. It was the custom in a defensive line of battle to protect the commander-in-chief. But the three ships astern of him, the French *Neptune* and the Spanish *San Justo* and *San Leandro*, had failed to do that duty by falling away to leeward. Lucas had bravely done it for them, and had been destroyed. Ahead of

Villeneuve, there were three ships of his own squadron. Two of them, the *Héros* and the *San Agustin*, bore away to leeward as soon as they were closely engaged. Only his next ahead, the *Santisima Trinidad*, stayed in her station. Admiral Dumanoir's squadron of seven ships, which was leading the line, continued to sail on to the northward, leaving another gap which grew steadily wider. So the *Bucentaure* and *Santisima Trinidad* were left alone, to windward of the rest of the fleet and straight in the path of Nelson's squadron.

And the *Santisima Trinidad*, by doing her duty and staying on course, had happened to put the *Bucentaure* in a position a sailing ship could not escape from. They were both close-hauled, and the enormous stern of the *Santisima Trinidad* was close under the

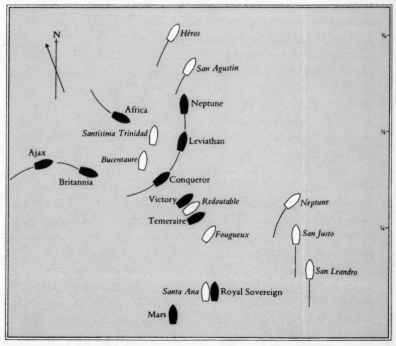

2 o'clock: Nelson's squadron

lee bow of the *Bucentaure*. Consequently, the *Bucentaure* could not alter course, to change the bearing of her guns: she could not turn to port without coming into the eye of the wind, and she could not bear away to starboard without falling foul of the ship ahead and probably losing her bowsprit. She might perhaps have backed her topsails and dropped astern, but it would have been a desperate measure in such a light breeze to lose what steerage way she had. So she was trapped and deserted, and became an almost helpless victim.

She never recovered from the first blast of the Victory's carronade and broadside. Or to go back further, she never really recovered from the discovery that her gunners could not aim when the ship was rolling. All her senior officers observed this with foreboding – Villeneuve himself, Captain Magendie and General Contamine – and the sight of the Victory bearing down on her in spite of all she could do seemed to them to show that the English knew their weakness.

She continued to fire as long as she could at ship after ship of Nelson's squadron, with her port broadside as the ships approached, and with her starboard broadside after they had passed; but as each of them passed her stern, the sickening destruction was renewed. The Leviathan brought to on her lee bow, and the Conqueror on her quarter, and kept her under fire; and the Britannia and the Ajax, entering the fight, attacked her at longer range from the windward side.

Within the smoke, it seemed to Villeneuve and his officers, as it did to men in most of the other ships, that they were fighting alone. For them, it was almost true. A chance breeze at the height of their battle made a momentary clearance, and Villeneuve observed that his rearguard was in chaos and his van still sailing north, away from the battle. At about 1.30 he hoisted a signal for the van to wear together. It was the last signal he ever made.

In the *Bucentaure*'s slow agony, most of Villeneuve's immediate companions fell. Captain Magendie, wounded in the mouth, had to go below to be bandaged: the first lieutenant took command of the ship and was severely wounded in the leg immediately after. The second lieutenant had to be called to command. Villeneuve's chief of staff, Captain Prigny, was carried below, and the ship's master, M. Gaudron – all officers who had been with him through the year. The ship's surgeons were totally overwhelmed by four hundred and fifty men in need of treatment, more than half of the crew. All the guns on the upper deck were destroyed and so was the rigging: the few men remaining up there had nothing more they could do, and Villeneuve sent them all below to save their lives. But he stayed on deck, pacing up and down like Nelson. If any man ever wanted to die in battle, and die bravely, that must have been his wish. He felt a personal responsibility for the men who were being killed all round him, and his staff heard him complaining bitterly that he of all men should be left alive. But nothing touched him.

At 1.40 the Conqueror shot away his main- and mizzen-masts. Unmanned, the *Bucentaure* fell off the wind: her bowsprit crashed into the stern of the *Santisima Trinidad*, and a moment later the foremast also fell. All three of the masts had fallen to starboard, and the wreckage covered the gunports and silenced the few of his guns which still remained. Somebody hoisted the flag on the stump of the mainmast, and it was observed that one of the two cadets entrusted with bearing the Imperial Eagle at the foot of the mast was still standing there, and had lashed the staff of the emblem round his waist.

Villeneuve was a man for whom fate always seemed to reserve a final blow, and now it happened again. Foreseeing some such disaster, he had ordered a rowing-boat to be towed astern, so that if the *Bucentaure* were lost he could be taken to another ship and hoist his flag in her. He sent for the boat, but it had vanished: it had sunk, or its tow-rope was shot away. The other boats on board were smashed to pieces by the gunfire and the falling of the masts. Without a mast, he could not make a signal; and if there was any French ship in sight, there was none that could possibly come to help him. As a last resort, he hailed the

Santisima Trinidad, to ask her to send him a boat, but nobody answered. His ship was wrecked, he was unhurt, and he could not get away. At 1.45, after one hour of close engagement, he accepted his ultimate disgrace and ordered his colours to be struck. The battered remains of the Eagle were thrown overboard.

The Conqueror sent her captain of Marines, James Atcherley, to take possession in a boat manned by only five men. When Atcherley reached her quarter-deck, Villeneuve proffered his sword, asking in English to whom he had the honour of surrendering. But Atcherley declined it, thinking that his captain was the proper person to disarm such a senior officer. Then he went down to the magazine, and symbolically locked it and put the key in his pocket. Passing　rough the gun decks, he saw frightful scenes of carnage: bodies lying in heaps along the middle of each deck, not merely dead but mangled again and again by the round shot and the splinters.

Atcherley left two of his men on board to take nominal charge of the ship – it was all he could spare. He embarked again in his small boat with Villeneuve, Magendie, Contamine and two of the admiral's staff. But the Conqueror had moved on, to engage the *Santisima Trinidad.* They rowed through the smoke, looking for a British ship, and found not the Victory but the Mars, which had drifted out of control across from the other battle, with her masts tottering and the headless body of Captain Duff still lying under a Union Jack on the gangway. So it fell to her first lieutenant, William Hennah, to receive the sword of the French commander-in-chief. He sent the prisoners down to the orlop, where Villeneuve could do nothing more but listen to the muffled sound of the guns destroying his fleet.

When the *Bucentaure* was dismasted, the *Santisima Trinidad* made sail to try to escape from the ring of enemies; and the men of the Conqueror, who saw her for the first time close at hand as she shook out the reefs in her topsails, marvelled at the size of her. Everything about her was bigger than any other ship – masts, sails, armament and hull. With 136 guns, she was a formidable sight; but she was also a most alluring prize. The Neptune and Leviathan had already damaged her in passing. The Conqueror came to on her quarter; and at the same time the Africa, sixty-four guns and one of the smallest ships of the British line, arrived from the northward, wore, and hove to on her weather bow.

Her crew was proportionately large: one thousand one hundred and fifteen men were aboard her, and she wore the flag of Rear-Admiral don Hidalgo Cisneros. Perhaps, although she was a flagship, the size of her crew had made her depend, even more than other Spanish ships, on desperate measures of recruitment. Certainly a very large proportion of this mass of men were soldiers and pressed men who had not been to sea until two days before. Like almost any man in any battle, they began to fight back as best they could when they found themselves under attack. But as soon as they saw that things were going wrong, they lost heart and started to panic, and the organization of the ship went to pieces.

She suffered the same disastrous fate as the *Bucentaure*. The two much smaller ships had placed themselves where she could hardly hit them, and they mercilessly shot her full of holes. They damaged her rigging, and the extra sail she set put too much strain on it. Suddenly, just after two o'clock, all her masts collapsed, the main- and mizzen- and then the foremast, and the whole majestic mass of sails, spars and rigging swayed and crumpled, and plunged into the water. A man in the Conqueror wrote that it was one of the most magnificent sights he had ever beheld. She ceased to fire, and lay there rolling like a monstrous log.

A few minutes later, one of the strangest scenes in the whole of the battle took place on her quarter-deck. Captain Digby of the Africa, the man who had already made his fortune in prize-money, was the first to get a boat away to take possession of this tremendous prize. He sent his first lieutenant, whose name was John Smith, with a small party of men. They climbed up her side and presented themselves among the wreckage of the quarter-deck. Admiral Cisneros, they found, had been wounded. So had his commodore, don Francisco de Uriarte, and the ship's captain, don I. Olaeta. Another officer received them with the greatest courtesy, but told them they were mistaken: the ship had not struck, but was still in action. John Smith was politely escorted back to the ship's side, and allowed to return with his men to the Africa.

The destruction of these two ships, one Spanish and one French, showed more clearly than any other encounter the reasons why the British won the day. First, there was the difference in seamanship. The *Bucentaure* and *Santisima Trinidad* had put themselves in a position where neither of them could manoeuvre without a risk of falling aboard the other: the Neptune, Leviathan, Conqueror and Africa, on the contrary, all sailed round them, perfectly under control in spite of the feeble breeze, and brought to in exactly the positions they had chosen. And the difference in gunnery: that could roughly be judged by the damage it did. The French and Spanish ships were left dismasted and in danger of sinking, while the British all remained in good order and sailed on to find themselves other victims. The Neptune had ten men killed, the Leviathan four, the Conqueror three, and the Africa – mostly in a later fight – had eighteen. But in the *Bucentaure* and *Santisima Trinidad*, the dead were uncountable: probably each had over two hundred. Perhaps twenty-five British dead all told, and perhaps four hundred French and Spanish: these macabre figures gave the measure of the skill in gunnery.

And the other thing this episode revealed was the different attitude of men in the three fleets. The British Belleisle, for example, was already dismasted and helpless, in a position not unlike the *Bucentaure*'s; but it simply never entered the mind of anyone on board her that she might strike her colours. The French also fought bravely, officers and crews, but surrender was always in their minds as a final solution if the battle went against them. The Spaniards showed a distinction between their officers and their men: some of the officers were as bravely determined as the French, but their crews were all inclined to lose their nerve and give up fighting as soon as they found what a horrible experience it could be.

With those three disadvantages among the French and Spanish – inferior ship-handling, vastly inferior gunnery, and an expectation of defeat – the battle could only be, as it was, a tragic one-sided affair.

By 2.15, one hour and a half after the Victory cut the line, one of Nelson's three battles, the attack on the centre, was all over. The *Bucentaure, Redoutable, Fougueux* and *Santisima Trinidad* were lying in ruin within a few hundred yards of each other. Nelson's two leading ships, the Victory and Temeraire, were damaged but were clearing their wreckage and getting under partial sail again. The remaining four of Villeneuve's squadron were retreating to leeward with the Neptune and Leviathan in pursuit, and one of them, the *San Agustin*, struck to the Leviathan at half past three. In the meantime, firing died down in the centre of the line and the smoke drifted away.

From the Victory, Hardy saw that Collingwood's squadron in the south was still vigorously fighting, while far in the north, a mile and a half away, the ships of the French and Spanish van were at last beginning to turn, apparently with the intention of joining the battle. 'I look with confidence to a victory,' Nelson had written in the memorandum, 'before the van of the Enemy could succour their rear; and then that the British Fleet would most of them be ready.' It had happened exactly. Six ships of his own squadron were still untouched, and four others were still in good order. Hardy signalled them to come to the wind on the port tack, which would put them as nearly as possible on a course to intercept the enemy van. And then he went down to the cockpit.

'Well, Hardy, how goes the battle?' Nelson asked him, shaking hands affectionately. 'How goes the day with us?'

'Very well, my Lord,' Hardy said. 'We have got twelve or

fourteen of the enemy's ships in our possession. But five of their van have tacked, and show an intention of bearing down upon the Victory. I have therefore called two or three of our fresh ships about us, and have no doubt of giving them a drubbing.'

'I hope none of our ships have struck, Hardy.'

'No, my Lord, there is no fear of that.'

Mr. Burke the purser had made a move to withdraw when the admiral and the captain started talking, but Nelson asked him to stay. Now he said: 'I am a dead man, Hardy. I am going fast: it will be all over with me soon. Come nearer to me. Pray let my dear Lady Hamilton have my hair, and all other things belonging to me.'

'I hope Mr. Beatty can hold out some prospect of life,' Hardy said.

'Oh, no,' Nelson said, 'it is impossible. My back is shot through. Beatty will tell you so.'

Hardy returned to the deck. Soon afterwards, he sent an officer by boat to tell Collingwood that Nelson was wounded.

It must have been alarming and dangerous to row through the middle of the battle, but the boat did not have very far to go. The ships in the centre had stopped, but those in the rearguard were still moving slowly north, and both fleets were gathering round the Victory. The Royal Sovereign had been a mile away when she started her engagement with the *Santa Ana*: now she was less than half that distance.

These two had fought the longest single fight in the battle. For over two hours they had been held together by their entangled rigging, hammering each other by gunfire. It could not have lasted so long if either of them had been free to give her whole attention to it; but both of them were also being harassed by other ships. Towards the end, the *Santa Ana*'s fire began to slacken, and soon after two o'clock it ceased. She drifted clear of the Royal Sovereign and fell off the wind, and her fore- and mainmasts went over the side. Ten minutes later, she struck her colours.

The Royal Sovereign was not in much better shape. All her

masts were wounded and she could not carry sail. Fifteen minutes after the *Santa Ana*'s, her main- and mizzen-masts fell. But she was still firing, and Collingwood, of course, had no intention of striking. He signalled for the Euryalus to come and take him in tow.

So it happened that when Hardy's boat arrived, Blackwood was there with Collingwood, and was also told the news. Hardy had not sent a message that Nelson was dying. Perhaps he was simply reluctant to say so, or perhaps he was being careful not to let Collingwood think that Nelson had relinquished the command. Knowing them both, he had tactfully given the impression that the message came from Nelson. 'When my dear friend received his wound,' Collingwood wrote in a letter afterwards, 'he immediately sent an officer to me to tell me of it, and give his love to me.' But in Beatty's recollection, Hardy took care that Nelson should not know that Collingwood had been told at all. 'Though the officer was directed to say that the wound was not dangerous,' Collingwood added, 'I read in his countenance what I had to fear.' Neither Collingwood nor Blackwood had any doubt of the truth; and Blackwood, who had parted from Nelson such a short time before, and could never have forgotten Nelson's last word to him, was desperately anxious to go back to the Victory in the hope of seeing him alive.

However, Collingwood sent him to the *Santa Ana* to accept the surrender of Admiral Alava. It was a curious thing, in the middle of battle, to send a ship's captain on a mission that could be fulfilled by a midshipman. Blackwood did not complain, but this was perhaps the sort of thoughtless order that made Collingwood unpopular with other officers. When Blackwood reached the *Santa Ana*'s deck, he was told that Alava was on the point of death. He chivalrously left him, as he thought, to die in peace, and only took away the captain of the ship, who had already delivered his sword on board the Royal Sovereign. But Alava, in fact, had only been knocked unconscious, and he recovered and lived to fight again.

*

Astern of the Royal Sovereign, eleven British ships and fourteen French and Spanish were fighting it out, almost all within range of each other. This was what Nelson had called a 'pell-mell battle': it was what he had hoped to bring about, and nothing quite like it had been seen before, or ever was seen again.

When Collingwood's squadron attacked in four separate groups, it cut the enemy line in three places – the fourth group coming up astern of the enemy rearguard. The line, such as it was, broke up. The ships round the Santa Ana were moving very slowly, so the rearguard, and Admiral Gravina's squadron of observation, were confronted by a fighting mass of ships ahead of them. Some held their course, and stood gallantly on into the mêlée, and some bore off to the eastward and sailed up the lee side of the battle, heading towards Cadiz and firing their port guns at any target they could see.

Here, even more than in the centre, the battle was like a lethal game, a mixture of skill and luck. The skill was in handling a ship so that her guns were bearing on enemies whose guns were not – that is to say, on the enemies' bows or sterns – and in avoiding enemies who were trying to do the same. The luck lay in the number of ships, all moving, all on different courses, and the smoke. In the slow evolutions of the two entangled fleets, every ship either sailed or drifted in and out of range of many others, and most of them, at some time, came under fire from three or four enemies at once. It is possible now for tacticians to work out roughly the movements of every ship, from the logs and reports that their captains and masters wrote. But nobody who was there had any clear view of what was happening. The gunners saw nothing except the square of sea and smoke which was framed by their own gunport: sometimes there was a ship in it flying an enemy flag, sometimes a friend, and once they were ordered to fire they went on firing at every enemy they saw. Captains steered as best they could, anticipating the movements of other ships and trying to avoid collisions: in the thick of it nobody wanted to fall aboard an enemy and lose his own steerage way. And upper-deck men, always under fire, set their sails as long as they could to suit the captains' courses, with rigging which was steadily shot away.

The first three in the battle, Royal Sovereign, Belleisle and Tonnant, were immobilized before the mass of the fleet bore down on them, and they had to endure it all without being able to manoeuvre. But they were still in action: they were still firing at anything that crossed their line of sight. While the Tonnant was aboard of Admiral Magon's flagship *Algésiras*, she was also engaged with two other ships, one French and one Spanish. Just after Magon struck, a lieutenant on the Tonnant's forecastle saw the Spaniard's flag come down. Somewhat innocently, he hailed her to ask her if she had struck. The answer shouted back was 'yes', and a strange little private drama took place in the heart of the battle.

This young man's name was Benjamin Clement. He went aft to the quarter-deck to tell the first lieutenant, who was in command since Captain Tyler was wounded, that the Spaniard had struck; and he was told to go and take possession of her. He pointed out that all the boats were shot, but he was told he must try. So he launched the jolly-boat: it was the smallest of boats that were carried on board, but the only one which looked as if it might float. And he embarked in it to board the Spanish ship, with a quartermaster and a Negro named Macnamara.

Before they had gone very far, a shot hit the stern of the boat and it turned upside-down; and Clement could not swim. But he had chosen two men who could. They stayed by him, and four seamen who saw what had happened jumped overboard from the Tonnant. They got Clement back to the side of the ship, and he put his leg through the boat's fall, which was still hanging down to the water. There, as the ship rolled, he was lifted into the air and then ducked in the sea again, and he thought he was drowning. Macnamara swam to the stern and came back with a rope and made it fast under Clement's arms, and he was hauled up and on board again through the stern port.* But that was the

* Clement kept in touch with Macnamara all his life, and left him a legacy when he died in 1836.

last of the boats, and the Tonnant's crew had the mortification of seeing another ship take possession of the prize. One of them described their own ship as drifting like a pig upon a grating, and as helpless as a sucking shrimp. But the Bellerophon came up astern of her, and took off the French ship which had been the third of her opponents, and gave her a few minutes' rest.

People believed in both fleets that gunfire stilled the wind, and that the breeze was consequently even lighter by this time than it had been in the morning. So, when the Bellerophon had cut the line astern of the Spanish *Monarca*, she had been moving so slowly that she fired her carronades three times and all her port guns at least twice as she passed. She hauled to the wind to fire again, but over the smoke she saw the top-gallant sails of another ship close on her starboard bow. She hauled all aback to check her way and avoid a collision. But she rammed the other ship and locked her foreyard into the other's mainyard. She was the French *Aigle*, which had had the Tonnant under fire.

Captain Cooke, who had thought he might be 'bowled out' and had shown the memorandum to Lieutenant Cumby and Mr. Overton the master, sent Cumby down to the gun deck with orders for the lieutenants at the guns. As Cumby came back along the main deck he met two sailors carrying Overton, whose leg was horribly shattered. And before he reached the quarter-deck ladder, another man told him the captain was wounded. When he reached Captain Cooke he was dead, shot in the chest by a musket-ball. Seamen said they had gone to raise him when he fell, and he had said: 'Let me lie a minute', and died at once. Suddenly, in the thick of the fight, Cumby was in command.

This fight was among the fiercest. The *Aigle* had a great many troops on board and was using musketry and hand-grenades, like the *Redoutable*; but she was also using her guns. The ships were so close that gunners fought hand to hand at the gunports, and seized each others' ramrods. At some of the ports, the French used muskets too, and at one they threw in a hand-grenade which set the gunners' storeroom on fire and blew open the door from the storeroom to the magazine. Luckily there were two doors with a passage between, and when it blew one open it blew the other shut, otherwise both the ships would have been demolished.

Men with buckets put out the fire without telling Cumby. He had enough to do on deck. He found the quarter-deck, poop and forecastle almost cleared of men by the musketry. It looked as if the *Aigle* would try to board. He called everyone down from the poop and mustered his own boarding-party under the half-deck – not because he had any hope of boarding, against the enemy's fire, but to repel them if they tried. And soon there were shouts of 'A l'abordage!' A crowd of Frenchmen started to swarm across, but the men below the half-deck shot them down. Five of them got on the spritsail yardarm and started to climb along it towards the bowsprit, but a seaman with presence of mind let go the spritsail brace which supported the end of the yard, and it tilted under their weight and they all fell into the water.

The hand-grenades were doing great destruction. In a classic gesture, Cumby picked one up while its fuse was burning and threw it overboard. But another scorched and wounded twenty-five of his upper-deck men; and one man, agonizingly hurt, ran aft and threw himself out of the stern port. The main topmast fell, and the sail dropped between the ships and hung like a curtain in front of the guns. It caught fire, and Cumby sent men to cut it away, dreading as all men did that the fire would spread.

On deck, the fight was going against him. He went below to walk round the gun decks and encourage the gunners; and someone remembered him saying that they had nothing else to trust except the guns, because the ship aloft was an unmanage-able wreck. The Bellerophon's gun decks were an especial hell, with musketry and hand-grenades added to their usual hazards. But those of the *Aigle* were worse. Fast gunnery was saving the situation. At last, the *Aigle* ceased firing from her lower deck and shut the ports of it. And the Bellerophon's gunners, relieved from attack, elevated their guns to shoot up through the enemy's deck. The *Aigle* hoisted her jib and drew herself clear under a final raking fire from the Bellerophon. She wore to go down to leeward, but she fell under the fire of another ship, the Defiance, and ten minutes later she struck. Deprived of her prize, Cumby looked round for another, and saw through the drifts of smoke that his first opponent, the *Monarca*, had also struck. He still had a boat, and sent some men to board her. That was all he could do. His own ship was out of control: the main and mizzen topmasts hanging over the side, and none of the running rigging in working order. There were no more opponents in range, so her firing ceased, and in the lull the surgeon sent Cumby a message: the cockpit was so crowded with wounded men that he could not operate there, and he asked for permission to bring some patients up to the captain's cabin for amputation.

Captain Churruca of the *San Juan Nepomuceno*, who had said his ship would never surrender unless he was dead, was one of those in the rearguard who bravely stood on into the thick of the fight. His fortune, after a few short encounters, was to meet the Dreadnought, which had been Collingwood's flagship. She was slow, and arrived in the battle late, and consequently all the more eager to secure a prize. And Collingwood, it was well known, had worked up her gunnery until it was reckoned the best in the British fleet. Churruca's makeshift crew stood never a chance against it. What he might have achieved by his threats and promises, and by his personal example, was never put to the test, for almost at once he was hit by a round shot which nearly severed his leg. He fell on the deck, tried to get up, and refused for some time to be treated or carried below. But the realization came to him that he was dying. He is said to have sent a message to his young wife, and to have ordered his colours to be nailed to the mast. But they were not. He died, and as soon as his death was known in the ship, his crew lost heart and surrendered. The fight had only lasted fifteen minutes.

By about 2.15, when Hardy went below to talk to Nelson, the end of Collingwood's battle was in sight. Some French and

Spanish ships were still resisting, but six of them had struck, and the rest were not fighting to win, but fighting to escape. An hour later five more had been captured, eleven in all of the sixteen which Collingwood cut off when he attacked the *Santa Ana*. Among them, many British ships were drifting, out of control and very badly damaged. The Royal Sovereign, Tonnant, Mars, Bellerophon and Belleisle were all unable to set a sail. But fresh ships, the slow sailers and those in the rear of the column, were still coming into action; and those which were damaged, far from striking their colours, signalled others to take them in tow, and laboured to clear the wreckage and get under way with whatever jury rig they could contrive. The Tonnant, without her top-gallant masts, succeeded in twenty minutes in cutting every-thing useless away, and in rigging topsails on her lower masts and top-gallant sails as topsails. But nothing could be quickly done about her rudder which the *Algésiras* had demolished. Her carpenter cobbled up a boat, and an officer went to Collingwood in it to ask for a ship to tow her. The Defiance was sent, and got a cable on board, and the Tonnant then hoisted a signal that she was ready for action again.

The Belleisle, without any masts at all, exhibited most sang-froid. Immovable, she fought for an hour whatever ships came her way, while her officers revived themselves by raiding the stock of grapes that Captain Hargood had kept in his cabin. At length, they saw a Spanish ship that had hoisted English colours, and they saw a chance to get themselves a prize. John Owen, the captain of Marines, took a boat with the ship's master and a few men in it, rowed across and climbed the Spaniard's side. She proved to be the *Argonauta*, which had been in action with the Achille, Swiftsure and Polyphemus. There was nobody alive on deck. Owen made his way across the quarter-deck, stepping over the bodies and the wreckage, and at the cabin door he met the ship's second captain, who gave him his sword and told him the captain was wounded and the crew had all gone below, out of the way of the shot. Owen returned the sword, and told him he should give it to Captain Hargood. He left the master in charge

of the prize and took the Spanish captain back to the wrecked
Belleisle, where Captain Hargood received the sword and
invited him into his cabin for a cup of tea.

So, by half past three, both the first two battles that Nelson
had foreseen had been decisively won. Twenty-five of the
French and Spanish ships had been engaged. Sixteen of them
had struck, and the rest, all more or less damaged, were crawling
away on the lee of the battle, trying to haul the wind towards
Cadiz. The van of the enemy had tacked, as Hardy had
observed at 2.15. But they were not yet in action, and they were
much too late.

In after years, while British critics argued over Nelson's
tactics, a fiercer argument raged among the French and Spaniards over the conduct of Admiral Dumanoir, who commanded
the van. For something like two hours after the battle began, he
sailed away from it; and when he did turn, of course it took him
nearly as long to sail back again. Naturally, the captains who
had fought and lost were furious, and called him a coward.
Some of them even blamed him for the whole disaster. Four
years later, he was court-martialled and exonerated; but the
court's decision did not stop the argument, and he never gave a
coherent explanation of why he acted as he did.

Villeneuve made two signals to bring him back. Soon after the
Victory cut the line, he hoisted a general order that all ships
which were not engaged should get into action as quickly as they
could. In his orders to the fleet he had written that this signal was
to be regarded as a disgrace by any ship it was addressed to –
and perhaps for that reason he did not address it to anyone. But
shortly before his masts came down he made the specific signal
to Dumanoir to wear. Dumanoir would not admit having seen
the first of these signals, and it was very probably hidden in the
smoke. But the second was repeated by the *Santisima Trinidad*,
and by some of the ships in his own squadron.

Afterwards he claimed that he ordered his squadron to tack,
and began to do so himself, before the second signal was made,
or at least before he saw it. And his claim is perhaps supported

by the fact that he tacked, while Villeneuve had ordered him to wear. But the claim only added to the argument: if he turned on his own initiative, why had he waited so long to do it? The original of his report, now in the archives of the French navy, still shows echoes of the criticism and disbelief he had to suffer all the rest of his life. In its margins an unknown hand wrote sarcastic comments in pencil. 'Preuve?' it notes at this claim; and underneath, 'Pas d'heure.'

To take a calm view, his strange and fatal delay would seem to have been an outcome of French naval tradition and training. British captains in battle were expected to make their own decisions, but the French were expected, on the whole, to act on orders from the commander-in-chief. It was a weakness, and some French captains knew it was, because flags were so often invisible in smoke. Dumanoir may be seen as a victim of this custom. All through those two hours he must have been in an agony of doubt. Common sense must have told him to turn as soon as Nelson's intention could be seen: yet the last order he had received had been to sail close-hauled which he was doing. Did Villeneuve still intend him to do so? Was there some reason for it? Was the van to avoid a battle and preserve its ships, as the fleet had avoided battle all those years? Or had he missed a signal in the smoke? It is said he had always mistrusted, mis-understood and disliked Villeneuve and resented his command: now he saw him going down in defeat; should he carry on doing what Villeneuve had told him, or attempt to rescue him and probably share his fate? The longer he waited, the less chance he had of helping. By the time he decided, it was a futile gesture, and he certainly knew he had no chance at all.

The manoeuvre itself was pathetically slow. Like other people, Dumanoir believed the gunfire had stilled the wind, although he was a mile and a half from any gunfire. The British fleet was still manoeuvring freely, but his squadron took nearly half an hour to change its course. Perhaps he happened to be in a patch of calm; but he had made the thing harder by ordering them to

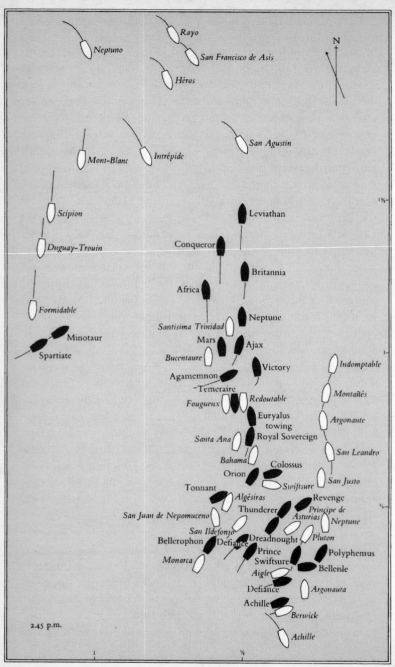

2.45: The last stage begins

tack instead of wear. In a very light breeze and a heavy swell, to tack was much the more difficult way to come about. His own flagship, the *Formidable*, tried it, and so did one of the others. But both of them lost their steerage way and had to launch boats to tow their heads round to the southward. All the others gave it up and wore, and so the squadron was scattered. Two of the French ships, the *Intrépide* and *Mont-Blanc*, ran foul of each other: one carried away her own jib-boom, and the other split her foresail. And two of the Spaniards, having wore, bore away to the eastward, leaving the squadron, and finally joined the ships of the centre and rear which were heading for Cadiz. One of these two was the *Rayo*; and she played the most ignominious part of any ship in the battle. Her captain, resplendently named Commodore don Enrique Macdonel, was really Henry Macdonnel, an Irishman born and bred, who had left his native country at the age of 16 with the patriotic intention of fighting against the English. A colourful career had brought him to the rank of commodore in the Spanish navy, and at last had given him his chance. But he had only just taken command of the *Rayo*, and she was old and rotten. He never succeeded in getting her up to windward, and she was the only ship-of-the-line at Trafalgar which did not fire a shot. Two days later her masts fell overboard, not through fighting but simply through wind and weather, and she drove ashore and was wrecked.

When Dumanoir at last got under way again he did not steer for the middle of the fight, but set a course to pass it half a mile to windward. To his dismay, he saw that only three of his seven ships were following him. All three of them were French. The two Spaniards had deliberately left him, and were going home. That left two, the *Intrépide* and the Spanish *Neptuno*. The *Intrépide*, Captain Infernet, set a course directly towards the *Bucentaure,* in a forlorn and gallant attempt to bring help to Villeneuve. And the *Neptuno*, after seeming to hesitate, followed him at a distance, heading towards the *Santisima Trinidad.*

By passing to windward, Dumanoir meant to cut off the rearmost ships of Nelson's squadron, which had not yet reached the battle: the Minotaur and Spartiate, in particular, were lagging behind the rest. This decision also angered his critics: 'To bring help to the Admiral,' the anonymous hand in the margin noted, 'there was no need to sail so close to the wind.' At best, it was a cautious line of action; and it turned out a total failure. As he sailed south, and the Minotaur and the Spartiate sailed east, they were almost on a collision course. But the Minotaur and Spartiate won. The Spartiate passed at pistol-shot ahead of the *Formidable* and fired a broadside into her bows, and both the British ships turned to port and engaged all four of the French ships as they passed. This brief encounter damaged the *Formidable* so much that her captain said she was only fit to sail down wind; and, being hit below the waterline as she rolled, she was making water faster than her pumps could clear it. To have borne down on the enemy at that moment, Dumanoir said, could only have added to the losses of the day. 'One always bears down,' the pencilled note replied, 'and succumbs gloriously.'

Very often in the next four years Dumanoir must have wished he had succumbed. But faced with the choice, he took the practical decision. An action that might have been glorious at noon would have been worse than useless at half past three. He stood on to the southward, exchanging a distant cannonade with the body of the British fleet. His long-range shots, into the close-packed groups of ships, damaged the French and Spanish captives as much as the British, and earned him more resentment from his countrymen. One shot from his squadron fatally wounded an English midshipman on board the *Redoutable*, and the remnants of Lucas's crew begged the British boarders to hide themselves below.

Captain Infernet of the *Intrépide* was a man of a different stamp. 'Where are you going?' Dumanoir is said to have shouted through his megaphone as Infernet altered course. 'Au feu,' Infernet shouted back, with a brevity one cannot match in English.

Infernet was a very large man of little education, who came from Provence and spoke a broad dialect. So, at least, he was described by one of his junior lieutenants. But the lieutenant, Gicquel des Touches, was a young aristocrat from the opposite end of France, and he may have exaggerated Infernet's provincialism, although he greatly admired his spirit as a captain. The lieutenant was 19; the captain was 50, and had spent forty years in the service, and he had on board his own son, who was 10.

Infernet had only been appointed to the *Intrépide* a week or two before in Cadiz, and so he had only been two days at sea with his crew. And the ship herself, he said, was the worst in the navy. She had been Spanish and was designed for eighty guns, but she was so weakly built that she could not carry guns of the normal calibres. Infernet made up for these shortcomings by his own heroic stature. 'Lay her head on the *Bucentaure*,' he bellowed in his hardly comprehensible Provençal, and he told his officers he intended to rescue Villeneuve and rally the ships that still remained fit to fight. It was an impossible project, and all of them knew it was. What he really meant to do was precisely what the critics said Dumanoir should have done: to bear down and succumb gloriously.

Among all the English who watched him coming with surprise and admiration was Captain Codrington of the Orion. He had arrived late and sailed into the mêlée somewhere well down the line astern of the Royal Sovereign. Codrington had a firm idea of how a battle should be fought, and he meant to fight it his way – to hold his fire until he found a perfectly suitable target. In his hunt for the target he sailed right through both fleets, complaining to his impatient officers that other British ships were getting in his way, and pointing out, like Lucas, that most of them were wasting their fire. He passed the Royal Sovereign and the Victory, and all the ships grouped round them, and found nothing there to fire at. He sighted a French ship and tried to close her, but the Ajax got there first, and then he bore down for the *Principe de Asturias*, but the Dreadnought crossed his line of fire and thwarted him again. At last, he came on the French *Swiftsure*, already damaged, and fired a broadside which dismasted her. Damaged only by the casual shot of both sides which was flying everywhere, he emerged at the northern edge of the fight; and there he met the *Intrépide* head-on. Even then, he felt he was being hindered by ships which were engaging her from a distance he thought too great. He backed all sail to get astern of the Ajax, and then made sail to pass across the head of the Leviathan, which was aboard the *San Agustin* and also firing on the *Intrépide*. 'I hope you will make a better fist of it,' the Leviathan's captain hailed; and Codrington sailed on, under the *Intrépide*'s stern and through her broadside, and came to on her bow.

Gicquel des Touches was in charge of the forecastle, and he had a boarding-party there. When he saw the Orion lying to the wind on his port bow, he sent a midshipman aft to ask Infernet to alter course and ram her, and he began to imagine himself in the heroic role of leading a boarding-party, and even of taking the Orion into Cadiz with the French flag flying above her own.

These thoughts were far from reality, for as the *Intrépide* approached the wreck of the *Bucentaure*, she was surrounded by enemies – seven at least within range. She did not alter course, and Gicquel des Touches went aft himself to find what had happened. The midshipman was lying on the gangway, overcome by fear of the shot that was flying from every side. He gave him a kick. On the poop he found Infernet brandishing a small curved sabre, which sliced off one of the wooden apples which decorated the rail. 'Do you want to cut my head off, Captain?' he asked facetiously. 'Not yours, my friend,' Infernet said, 'but the head of the first man who says surrender.' Beside him was a colonel of infantry, distinguished at the Battle of Marengo, who seemed to be troubled at the situation and to be trying to hide behind the captain's massive body. 'What's the matter, Colonel?' Infernet shouted. 'Do you think I am wearing armour?' And he roared with laughter.

But of course he had to surrender. His masts came down and

his rudder was shot, and then he struck his colours – the last of the French or Spanish flags to be flown in that part of the battle. Codrington took him on board the Orion, and his son went with him.

The Victory and Temeraire, lying close together, both reopened fire as Dumanoir passed the centre of the fleet, and down in the cockpit the roar and concussion of the guns began again. 'Oh Victory, Victory, how you distract my poor brain!' Nelson was heard to say in the loneliness of his pain and approaching death. And a little later, he added as if in surprise: 'How dear is life to all men.' He had made Beatty leave him to see to the other wounded, but in face of the prayers and hollow hopes of Burke and Scott, he seemed to want somebody to admit that he was dying, in order perhaps that he could compose his mind by discarding any doubt. He asked for Beatty again. 'Ah, Mr. Beatty,' he said when Scott had fetched him, 'I sent for you to say, what I forgot to tell you before, that all power of motion and feeling below my breast are gone. And *you* very well know I can live but a short time.' 'My Lord, you told me so before,' Beatty said. Nelson, he thought, was now remembering a man who had been fatally injured on board some months before, and had had those symptoms. He examined Nelson's feet and legs. 'Ah, Beatty, I am certain of it. Scott and Burke have tried it already. You *know* I am gone.' At last Beatty said: 'My Lord, unhappily for our country, nothing can be done for you.' And he turned away and withdrew a few steps to hide his feelings. 'I know it,' Nelson said; and later, 'God be praised, I have done my duty.'

Beatty asked if his pain was very great, and Nelson said it continued so very severe that he wished he was dead. Then, in a lower voice, he said: 'Yet one would like to live a little longer.' And after a pause of a few more minutes he added in the same tone: 'What would become of my poor Lady Hamilton if she knew of my situation?' Scott and Burke fanned him with pieces of paper, and rubbed his chest, and offered him lemonade. And all round, in the darkness of fifty orlop decks, other men lay dying, each in his own unapproachable solitude.

Right down at the other end of the fleet, another final drama was being played. The French *Achille* had been fighting with musketmen in her tops, and she had suffered the penalty Nelson predicted for that kind of warfare: she had set her own mizzen top on fire. She wore out of the battle and stood down wind, but she did not strike, and some British ships followed her down – among them the Prince, which had only just arrived and was fresh to battle. The *Achille* had fought with a number of ships, including her namesake the British Achille; and so hard had the fighting been that four of her officers had successively taken command, each falling wounded. The lieutenant in charge of the upper gun deck was acting as captain when she was found to be burning.

A fire in the top was more of a threat than anything an enemy could do. Without orders, but with a general accord, officers and men abandoned the upper-deck guns and began to hack down the mast, hoping to let it fall overboard, while the lower batteries continued firing. But the Prince fired two broadsides, and the second brought down not only the mizzen but all three masts at once. They fell fore and aft along the centre of the deck, the burning mizzen top fell on the boats amidships and the main-mast crushed the fire pump. Red-hot wreckage fell through to the decks below, and very soon the fire was out of control. Everyone who could move came up on deck: a few of the wounded were carried or dragged themselves, but most of them were left below on the orlop. They threw overboard all the debris that would float, and some hundreds of men jumped into the sea.

This was a maritime disaster quite different from the necessities of battle. The *Achille* had still not struck her colours, and she never did so. But the ships that had attacked her immediately ceased their fire and did all they could to help her. The Prince stood away to escape the explosion which was the only possible end for a ship on fire, but she launched her boats and their crews rowed in to save the French, at imminent peril of their lives. The schooner Pickle and the cutter Entreprenante bore down to help the rescue. Boats from the Belleisle and Euryalus joined in, and between them they took two hundred and fifty men from the water.

At about 4.15 the Victory hoisted a signal to come to the wind on the starboard tack. This was the signal that ended the last scattered shots in the battle: it implied that the ships which were still in pursuit should break off the chase and return towards the flagship. It was all over. The greater part of both fleets lay grouped round the Victory and Royal Sovereign, drifting very slowly, and rolling in the swell. Eighteen ships had struck, and the *Achille* had burned nearly down to the waterline with her ensign still flying on the poop. To the north-east, Admiral Gravina was escaping with ten ships towards Cadiz, and to the south-west, Dumanoir with his four was disappearing towards the open sea.

In the Belleisle, Paul Nicolas, the 16-year-old lieutenant of Marines, who had been so appalled five hours before by the first of the round shot, was still alive and unhurt, but mentally and physically exhausted; and his feelings, young as he was, were probably typical of the survivors in the British fleet. There was not so much triumph as he expected. People were asking each other about their friends, and almost everyone had a friend who was dead or wounded. Nicolas went down to the gunroom, where two of his fellow officers were lying dead: one was the first lieutenant who had said at breakfast that he thought he was going to die. And he went to the cockpit to ask about other companions. The sight and sound of it shocked him more than the battle. It seemed to him a vault of misery: shrieks and groans were echoing in it. Benches and deck were covered with mutilated men: the ship had ninety-six wounded. Several were lying on the long table waiting the surgeon's attention, and one was undergoing amputation. What a contrast, he thought, to the hilarity he had seen round that table the night before, for the cockpit was where the midshipmen lived on board.

The upper deck was almost equally dreadful: masts, yards, sails, ropes, splinters, bits of wreckage and mangled corpses – it was like a shipwright's yard covered with blood. People were starting to heave the bodies overboard.

He was called to the cabin to join Captain Hargood and the Spanish captain at their tea. All the officers assembled, smoke-blackened and dirty. Hargood noticed that Owen the captain of Marines was wounded, and he sent for the surgeon who came up reeking with blood and doctored their minor hurts. They talked about the officers who were dead, remembering the best things about them and forgetting the worst. And all of them told each other their own recollections of the battle, as people do after such an emotional strain. Everyone, like Nicolas, was exhausted. They needed rest and some food and talk before they started the gruesome job of tidying up the mess. It was calm, the enemy had fled, there was nothing urgent to do – except on the orlop decks throughout the fleets, where the surgeons were busy at their trade, peering into wounds by the light of tallow candles held by their assistants.

Hardy went down to the orlop again about four o'clock, when it was clear that Dumanoir would not be able to offer a serious threat. He congratulated Nelson on a complete victory: he did not know how many of the enemy were captured because he could not see them all distinctly, but he was sure of fourteen or fifteen. 'That is well,' Nelson said, 'but I bargained for twenty.' Then he said emphatically: 'Anchor, Hardy, anchor.'

'I suppose, my Lord, Admiral Collingwood will now take upon himself the direction of affairs.'

'Not while I live, I hope, Hardy!' Nelson said, and he tried to raise himself from the bed. 'No, do *you* anchor, Hardy.'

'Shall *we* make the signal, sir?' Hardy asked him.

'Yes. For if I live, I'll anchor.'

That insistence that the fleet should anchor was difficult for

Hardy, who knew he would very soon be under Collingwood's command. And later, when it was publicly known, it was a source of criticism of Collingwood – for neither he nor Hardy did make the signal to anchor. It was the last order Nelson gave; people found it hard to admit that he could have been mistaken, and argued that if it had been faithfully obeyed, later events would have turned out more happily than they did. But this was to honour Nelson's memory too highly. He was out of touch; but Hardy and Collingwood were second to none in seamanship, and knew what they were doing.

After this, Nelson's thoughts reverted to himself and the love and friendship he was relinquishing. He spoke again in a lower tone, and told Hardy he felt in a few minutes he would be no more. 'Don't throw me overboard.'

'Oh, no, certainly not.'

'Then you know what to do,' Nelson said. 'And take care of my dear Lady Hamilton, Hardy. Take care of poor Lady Hamilton. Kiss me, Hardy.'

The captain knelt down and kissed his cheek. 'Now I am satisfied. Thank God I have done my duty.'

Hardy stood for a minute or two in silence, and then he knelt down again and kissed his forehead. 'Who is that?' Nelson asked.

'It is Hardy.'

'God bless you, Hardy.'

Hardy withdrew, and went back to the quarter-deck. Shortly after, Nelson's breathing became harder, and his voice faint. He said to Scott: 'Doctor, I have not been a *great* sinner.' And after a short pause, 'Remember that I leave Lady Hamilton and my daughter Horatia as a legacy to my country. And never forget Horatia.' Last of all, Scott heard him whisper distinctly, 'Thank God I have done my duty.'

One of the last of the shots from Dumanoir's squadron cut the cable by which the Euryalus was towing the Royal Sovereign. Neglecting Collingwood's order, Blackwood wore ship and stood for the Victory, desperately eager to see his friend before he died. On the Victory's gangway they told him Nelson was still alive, but when he reached the cockpit he was dead. Only the faithful Scott and Burke and the two servants had been present. An unknown hand made the pencil entry in the Victory's log: 'Partial firing continued until 4.30, when a victory having been reported to the Right Hon. Lord Viscount Nelson, K.B., and Commander-in-Chief, he died of his wound.' That night Blackwood wrote to his wife that in his life he had never been so shocked or so upset: on such terms, it was a victory he never wished to have witnessed.

STORM

At ten minutes to six the *Achille* exploded and a mushroom cloud rose into the evening air. The British boats, out of danger now, went closer in to collect the last survivors. Among them was a black pig, swimming strongly, and a naked young woman clinging to a spar. The pig was captured by the Euryalus and eaten that evening. The woman was taken to the Pickle, and given a jacket and trousers, and then she was transferred with fifty rescued men to the Revenge. There, she roused everyone's gallantry and became a kind of mascot. A lieutenant gave her some sprigged blue muslin he had found in a Spanish prize, and the captain ordered two shirts from the purser's store to make her a petticoat. Her name, she said, was Jeanette: her husband had been in the crew, and she had stowed away in disguise. In the disaster she could not find him, and she was left with the wounded on the orlop. She waited there until the deck above was burning and the guns came crashing through it. Then she climbed out of a gunroom port and sat on the rudder chains. But molten lead from the rudder stock dripped down on her. She took off her clothes and jumped into the sea, and found a broken spar with men clinging to it, but one of them bit and kicked her until she had to let go and find another. However, her story had a happier ending; for a few days later, her husband was found among the prisoners.

In a day when destruction and death had been commonplace, it was odd incidents like these that people talked about. Of events in the battle, what stuck most firmly in their minds was the occasional strange behaviour of wounded men. They were used to gunnery, and to sailing in difficult circumstances, and those who had never been shot at before had found, as most people do, that they were not so cowardly as they had feared. 'When they had given us one duster,' a sailor wrote, 'and I found myself snug and tight, I bid fear kiss my bottom, and set to in good earnest.' But none of them had seen the effects of wounds and shock on such a scale. They told of a man who had his arm smashed and walked down to the cockpit and sang 'Rule Britannia' all through the amputation. In the Bellerophon, Cumby met a messmate waiting for the surgeon, and said he was sorry to see him wounded. ''Tis only a mere scratch,' the officer replied, 'and I shall have to apologize to you by and by for leaving the deck on so trifling an occasion.' He was waiting, it turned out, to have his right arm amputated. In the Revenge, the ship's cobbler, a merry man and a celebrated dancer, was serving a gun when a shot came in at the port and killed the crew. Men bundled the corpses out of the port. But when the cobbler was half-way out, he began to kick, and they hauled him back in time. 'A good thing I showed you some dance steps,' he said soon after, without the least ill-will, 'otherwise I would have been snug in Davy Jones's locker.' In the Tonnant, there was a more macabre story: a man who had had his leg taken off by the surgeon heard some cheering from the gun deck up above, and he joined in and cheered so loudly that he burst the ligatures and died of the consequent haemorrhage.

Telling each other stories like these – proud of success, grieving over friends, glad to be alive, counting the prize-money and planning how they would spend it – they were all perhaps more shaken and weary than they knew. Work went slowly. As the evening advanced they began in an almost leisurely way to repair their own damage, and take in tow the ships that could not be repaired, and the prizes they had won.

Among men in this mood, already emotional, the news of Nelson's death caused a unique and overwhelming shock. Hardy himself went to the Royal Sovereign to tell Collingwood, and formally hand over the command. Collingwood was seen in tears. It was in the Royal Sovereign too that a sailor wrote home: 'Our dear Admiral Nelson is killed! so we have paid pretty sharply for licking 'em. I never set eyes on him, for which I am both sorry and glad; for, to be sure, I should like to have seen him – but then, all the men in our ships who have seen him are such soft toads, they have done nothing but blast their eyes, and cry, ever since he was killed.'

And in every ship that left any record, it was the same. An officer from the Tonnant who went to report to Collingwood saw the expressions on people's faces and guessed at once what had happened: no other conceivable event could have caused such sadness. A boat from the Entreprenante brought the news to the Belleisle: all work on board came to a halt, and tears ran down the faces of veteran seamen. Some ships were not told, but after nightfall they saw the Victory was in darkness, and the commander-in-chief's night signal was carried by the Euryalus, which had returned to tow the Royal Sovereign: they could not bring themselves to believe what that implied. By some strange chance, the Temeraire, which had been closest to the Victory in action, was the only one which neither knew nor guessed until several days had passed. Hardy, Collingwood, Blackwood, Scott, all the senior officers in the fleet, were mourning the best of friends: humbler people felt as if they had lost a parent – 'as great a hero as ever existed', a young lieutenant wrote, 'a seaman's friend, and the father of the fleet'. People of every kind who wrote letters expressed the same emotion – not mainly respect or admiration, but love: 'our beloved Admiral', 'our dear Admiral Nelson', 'a friend I loved'. The word love can never have been used so universally about any man among men. A kind of warmth was extinguished in the fleet, and many other people had the same thought as Blackwood: it had been a glorious victory, but it was Nelson's victory; it was worth the loss of lives, which victories always cost, but it was not worth the loss of Nelson.

Collingwood took over command, and moved to the Euryalus: the Royal Sovereign had no mast to hoist his signals. It had been hard for him to relinquish command to Nelson and suffer the captains' comparisons, but it was far harder to take it up again. Everyone admired the way he had led into battle, but afterwards in the eyes of most of the captains he could do nothing right. Whatever he did, they asked themselves and each other what Nelson would have done.

And no admiral in history ever had a harder fleet to manage. It was huge, over fifty ships, and half of them dismasted. His first orders were to take the disabled ships in tow. The frigates, and the ships that had been late in battle and survived with masts intact, all got a cable on board a ship that could not move. The Thunderer took the *Santa Ana*, the Prince took the *Santisima Trinidad*, the Naiad frigate took the Belleisle, the Spartiate took the Tonnant – and during the evening, very slowly, the mass of ships got under way to the southward. Gibraltar was their only port of refuge.

The breeze was still westerly and very light, and a great swell was running. In those conditions towing was difficult and dangerous. Even Blackwood and his crew were in trouble. Their log recorded: 'At 7.36 took aback, and the Royal Sovereign fell aboard of our starboard beam, and there being a great swell she damaged the main channels, took away the lanyards of the main and mizen rigging, jolly-boat from the quarter and davits, the most of the quarter-deck and waist hammock cloths, boards, railing, with a number of hammocks and bedding; took away the main and mizen top-gallant masts, lost the royals and yards. Tore the fore and main sails very much, and took away a main part of the running rigging. At 7.40 got her clear.' In the dark, they worked to repair this damage. At nine, they sounded in 23 fathoms, and Collingwood made the general signal to prepare to anchor. Twenty minutes later, the sounding was down to 13 fathoms. Uncertain of his position off the Trafalgar shoals, he made the signal to wear, and he came to the wind on the port tack, a course of about north-west, to stand away from the land.

At dawn forty-four ships were in sight, but they were widely scattered and mostly inshore of the flagship. The wind was rising. Collingwood cast off the Royal Sovereign and ordered the Neptune to take her in tow. He sent the Pickle and Entreprenante with orders for other ships to close round the Neptune, and under his orders Blackwood stood back towards Cape Trafalgar to round up the rest of the fleet. By noon the Euryalus's log was recording strong gales and heavy rain. And now began an ordeal far harder than the battle: the storm, rising to hurricane, which blew for seven days straight in to the hostile shore.

The logs of the ships had been sparse in their recording of the battle, but when the storm began they had an unstudied eloquence which, even through its ancient technicalities, can still evoke a scene of nightmare danger. For the most part, it was the masters or the officers of the watch who wrote up the logs. They were not experienced at describing battles, but they could precisely describe the problems of seamanship, and wherever one cares to look at the notes they made, one sees between the lines an image of seas breaking over the decks, and driven rain and spindrift, and men working aloft in wildly rolling ships on masts and rigging already damaged by shot and hastily spliced and knotted – and, above all, the menace of a lee shore.

Euryalus at midnight: 'Strong gales and rain with heavy squalls. The fore topmast staysail split and blown away by a heavy squall from the westward. At 2, sounded in 45 fathoms. At 4, sounded in 65 fathoms. At 5.30, out 3rd reef of the topsails and swayed them up.'

Victory: 'Bent a main topsail, old one shot to pieces. Got a jib-boom up and rigged for a mizen mast. Carpenters employed stopping the shot holes . . . Got up a jury fore topmast, and a main top-gallant yard for a fore topsail yard . . . At 4.15, heavy squalls. At 5.10, carried away the main yard. Split the main topsail and mainsail all to pieces. Cleared away the wreck. At daylight saw the Royal Sovereign with signal 314 flying [ship is in distress and in want of immediate assistance].'

Royal Sovereign: 'At 5.30 our foremast went by the board,

and with it all the sails, standing and running rigging. Cleared the wreck. At 5.40 carried away the towrope. Rigged a jury foremast and fired several guns to windward and leeward, and sounded every half hour. Lost overboard one of the poop carronades by the violent rolling of the ship.'

Naiad frigate: 'Took the Belleisle in tow, she being without a mast or bowsprit . . . At 5, parted the stream cable in towing the Belleisle. At 7.40, strong breezes with continual rain. The Belleisle fell on board us, endeavouring to take her in tow. Damaged the jolly boat and carried away the greater part of the starboard quarter gallery. Could not accomplish it by boats, the sea running so high. At 12, squally with rain. At 12.30 [a.m.] carried away the larboard main topsail sheet, and the leech and rope at the 2nd reef gave way, and the sail split across. Cut away the leech and topsail sheet to save the yard. The sail went overboard; the fore topmast staysail went in pieces. At 5.40 saw the Belleisle very near the shore to the eastward of Cape Trafalgar. Made sail and stood towards her. At 7.10, more moderate. Sent a boat alongside the Belleisle and took her in tow. Made sail.'

Entreprenante cutter: '[During the battle] preserved from different wrecks, &c., upwards of 169 men . . . Hard gales with heavy sea. Split the mainsail. Lost best part of it. Set the trysail and storm jib. At noon, wore ship. Shipped several very heavy seas. Made several signals of distress. P.M. – Stormy with heavy seas, several of which broke in upon the decks. Thought it necessary for the preservation of the cutter to heave 5 guns overboard, besides shot, remains of the old mainsail, hammocks, &c., to lighten her, being nearly waterlogged. Split the foresail and storm jib.'

The Swiftsure had taken Captain Lucas's *Redoutable* in tow at the end of the battle and put a prize-crew of fifty men on board. They worked all night at the pumps with the help of a few of the French survivors, and did what they could to stop the leaks, cover the open gunports and shore up the poop, which was on the point of collapse. The gun decks remained full of bodies and debris. Lucas was still on board, and observed that no night had ever been more laborious: he was also pleased to see that some of his men were hiding weapons on the orlop deck, intending, they said, to recapture the ship. The next morning the Swiftsure wisely sent a boat and took him off, with his first lieutenant. At noon, when the wind was rising, the *Redoutable*'s last mast went overboard, and that evening in the gale the prize-crew made signals of distress.

'Hove to, and out boats,' the Swiftsure's log recorded, 'and brought the prize officer and his people on board, and a great many of the prisoners. At a quarter past, the boats returned the last time with very few in them, the weather so bad and sea running high that rendered it impossible for the boat to pass. Got in the boats. At a quarter past ten, the *Redoutable* sunk by the stern.'

Lucas watched, and admitted how difficult this gallant rescue had been: the boats brought off one hundred and sixty-nine of his men, one hundred and thirty-four of them more or less severely wounded. He believed that the greater part of his host of wounded had got up to the poop, but he could not have seen them and his survivors must have exaggerated: the orlop deck was the safest place in battle, but in a sinking ship it was a trap. To drag some hundreds of men with shattered limbs up a series of ladders in the pitch darkness of a rolling ship at night was well-nigh impossible, and perhaps a mistaken kindness. In the *Redoutable*, and in many sinking ships in the next few days and nights, innumerable men who could not move were left to lie below as the water rose; and there they drowned comparatively quickly. But fifty wounded men of the *Redoutable* did get overboard and survived the night in the sea. 'At half past three,' the Swiftsure wrote, 'heard the cries of some people. Out boats, and picked up part of the crew of the prize that had saved their lives on a raft, and at daylight saw two other rafts with people on them and saved them. Served shirts to those that were naked.'

*

In the same night, the flagship *Bucentaure* broke adrift from her tow and began to drive down towards the shore. On board she had two English officers and a few men, together with all the survivors of her own officers and crew and all the bodies of the dead. Still on board were Captain Prigny, wounded, who had been Villeneuve's chief of staff, and the ship's first lieutenant, who was unwounded and had taken command in the final stage of the battle. These senior officers decided, correctly enough, to retake the ship and try to save her – for the few English had made no progress in clearing the wreckage or getting any sail on her. Prigny, lying in his cabin, sent for the English officers and asked them to surrender voluntarily, in order to save any further loss of life. They agreed, and during the next few hours the French cut away the mizzen-mast and its rigging, which had fallen on deck; and they lashed a top-gallant mast to the stump of the mizzen and set a single sail. Under that, they drove at five knots towards Cadiz.

It was black night. In the driving rain there was nothing to be seen. They only roughly knew their position, from a doubtful fix they had taken the day before. There was a local fisherman on board, and three men who said they had been pilots, and the first lieutenant left the wheel to them.

At last they saw the light of Cadiz, and began to hope. But soon after there was a violent crash. She had struck a rock. It dismounted the rudder, which began to shake the stern frame to pieces and threatened to split the ship open. They sounded in 7½ fathoms, and let go the only two anchors they had. Still hoping to save the ship, they cut the rudder away, and threw everything movable overboard, including the ship's provisions; they broached all the casks of water, wine and brandy, and pumped the mixture overboard with the bilge pumps. But in the troughs of the waves, the stern was grounding, and the water started to gain on the pumps. A boat came down from a French ship that was still under command, and asked what help they needed: anchors and warps, they said, and boats to stream them with. But nothing came, only another boat in which they began to disembark the wounded. The hold flooded, the water rose to the orlop, and Prigny gave the order to abandon. By luck and skill, they got everybody off, leaving only the hundreds of corpses; and with that macabre cargo, the *Bucentaure* broke up.

In the Euryalus, Collingwood sailed round and round the scattering fleet, bombarding the ships with signals: sometimes in a single hour Blackwood's hardworking signalmen hoisted ten for him. No doubt he felt he had to take an active command of a situation that grew worse and worse. But in retrospect it is hard to think that Nelson's captains needed so often to be told what they should do. Certainly some of them, using a lifetime's training to save their ships and their lives, were annoyed by trivial orders. What they had to do was starkly simple. At any time, the ships that were still intact could have saved themselves, by weathering Cape St. Vincent and giving themselves sea-room in the Atlantic, or possibly by beating down to Gibraltar. But none of them could do so, close-hauled to the gale, while they had others in tow. It was out of the question to abandon a disabled British ship, and no captain, except in a last extremity, would abandon the prizes that meant a life of wealth. There was no option except to continue to claw off the land, or to anchor, until the wind changed or moderated. And many of them, including the Victory, could not anchor because their anchors were lost or their cables cut by shot.

Blackwood was with Collingwood through it all, and he was the only man who judged him charitably. Perhaps the grief they were sharing had brought them together; but Blackwood, one cannot doubt, was an exceptionally charitable man. Every second day, whatever happened, he wrote a long letter to his wife: 'Wednesday 23rd. Last night and this day, my dearest Harriet, has been trying to the whole fleet, but more so to the Admiral who has the charge. It has blown a hurricane, but, strange to say, we have as yet lost but one ship – one of our finest prizes – La Redoutable; but which I feel the more, as so many poor souls were lost . . .' And two days later: 'All yesterday and last night the majority of the English fleet have been in the most perilous state; our ships much crippled, with damaged prizes in tow; our crews tired out, and many thousand prisoners to guard; all to be done with a gale of wind blowing us right on the shore . . . Could you witness the grief and anxiety of Admiral Collingwood, (who has done all that an admiral could do,) you would be very deeply affected . . . I am happy that I have been able to render him any service, and had he not come on board here, even our own fleet might not have been saved. From the disabled state of most of the ships, they could not be collected, so that we have been doing nothing else but running to all points, the ship covered with signals, to try and get them together, and off from the shore, in which I hope at last we shall succeed.'

'The French commander-in-chief Villeneuve is at this moment at my elbow,' Blackwood went on: for Villeneuve also had to endure the whole storm and watch the further destruction of his fleet. The Mars, to which he had first been taken, had no captain and was hardly fit to sail, so she handed him over to the Neptune, where he was entertained by Captain Fremantle, the most insular of Englishmen. Fremantle laughed heartily at what he called the gasconade of General Contamine and the admiral's aides-de-camp, who he said were true Frenchmen; but to his own surprise, he found Villeneuve 'a very pleasant and Gentlemanlike man, the poor man was very low'. After two days he sent Villeneuve to the Euryalus and kept the others. Blackwood was a more cosmopolitan companion: he spoke French very well, he had liked Decrès, and he understood Villeneuve's misfortunes. Collingwood detested the French on principle, but even he thought Villeneuve a well-bred man and a very good officer: 'He has nothing in his manners of the offensive vapouring and boasting which we, perhaps too often, attribute to Frenchmen.' Possibly, in those terrible days in the Euryalus, Villeneuve had a glimpse of a navy in which he could happily have served.

*

On the second afternoon of the storm the wind dropped a little, and Collingwood was given a new source of worry: several enemy ships were seen coming out of Cadiz. He hastily signalled seven or eight of his ships which were still intact and still in sight to form a line of battle, and some of them slipped their tows to do it. But the French and Spanish had not come out to fight; they had come in the hope of picking up some of the captured ships that were drifting. The expedition was led and inspired by the French Captain Cosmao of the *Pluton*, who had taken a very active part in the battle: the rest of his ships were those that had lagged to leeward and avoided most of the fight – the French *Neptune* and *Héros*, and the Spanish *San Justo*, *Rayo* and *San Francisco de Asis*. By any standards, to sally forth in the teeth of the storm was a brave attempt, and the British watched it with appreciation. But it brought no profit. They escorted two disabled ships into harbour, the Spanish *Neptuno* and Collingwood's own opponent the *Santa Ana*. But the *Neptuno* was wrecked in the bay as she entered, and the *Rayo* foundered outside it.

After the tow-rope parted between the Naiad and Belleisle, the ships lost each other in the darkness. The crew of the Belleisle had worked all day to get up jury masts, and by night they had a few small sails set on them. With those they tried to steer a south-easterly course in the hope of clearing Cape Trafalgar. But they knew the wind and sea were taking them down to leeward, and all that night they expected to go aground.

Paul Nicolas was too tired to stay on his feet. He turned in, in a cot in the wardroom, for the midshipmen's berth was full of wounded. At midnight a message came for all officers to report on deck: the captain believed the ship would soon be ashore. He jumped up, and there was a crash: everyone thought she had struck. But it was a 24-pounder gun which had broken adrift from its lashings on the deck above. With difficulty, he got on deck. The ship was labouring, and the sea was coming in through the upper-deck ports and over the hammock nettings.

Round shot had fallen out of the racks and was rolling from side to side of the deck among men who were lying there exhausted.

All night they counted the hours, knowing that dawn would show them whether they were to live or die. Nicolas was frankly terrified. He thought of home, and family and friends, and he was in despair. The battle had been a fair risk, with a chance for everyone, but shipwreck in a hurricane was certain death to all. Whenever the clouds lightened, he thought it was dawn, and when the darkness fell again his weary hope fell further into despondency. At last the order came to strike two bells, which was five o'clock. Men roused themselves and stared towards the shore. Someone shouted: 'Land on the lee bow! Put the helm up!' Instantly all was bustle and confusion. Very slowly, the ship's head came round under her makeshift sail. The breakers were a mile to leeward, throwing up spray to a terrific height. But the Naiad was still in sight and she bore down to the very edge of the shoals and hauled the Belleisle off.

Any dismasted sailing ship has a quick and vicious motion, and that was agony for the wounded. They were helplessly rolled about the decks or, if hammocks had been rigged for them, they swung and bumped against each other and the bulkheads. As they were thrown about, their wounds broke out afresh and hundreds of them bled to death. In the Tonnant, sixteen men had amputations, and only two of them survived the storm.

In the Victory, before the storm was at its height, Dr. Beatty turned his attention from the wounded to the problem of preserving Nelson's body. Such a problem was unfamiliar. Since time out of mind, men who died at sea had been hove overboard, or in the formal phrase 'committed to the deep'. Neither Beatty nor anyone else had equipment or knowledge for embalming, and there was no lead on board to make an air-tight coffin. So he chose a leaguer, which was the largest kind of cask. He cut off the hair and made a brief autopsy, and then the body was put in the cask and the cask was filled with brandy. Standing on end, it was lashed securely on the middle deck and watched by a sentinel.

Conditions were much the worst in the dismasted prizes, because they had far more wounded than their surgeons could hope to attend. And in mental stress the British officers in the prizes suffered most of all. Some had been hastily put on board with a dozen men, and found themselves adrift and facing death among hundreds of foreign sailors. And in some of the prize-crews, the British discipline broke down. In the aftermath of the battle, commanded only by a junior lieutenant, men rightly believed that whatever they did would be forgotten, and they found the enemy's stocks of wine and brandy. In the *Monarca* a couple of officers were commanding a sinking ship with five hundred prisoners on board and fifty-five Englishmen, mostly drunk; and one of the officers, a midshipman, said afterwards that he had not been afraid in the battle but was very afraid in the prize.

Probably most of the French and Spanish officers thought of retaking their ships. As they had struck their colours, it was against the custom of war, but in these conditions nobody could blame them. The *Bucentaure*'s officers had done it but failed to save the ship; and in Admiral Magon's flagship *Algésiras* they also tried.

The Tonnant had put a prize-crew on the *Algésiras* as soon as she struck, but nobody took her in tow. Magon was dead and her captain was wounded, but all the officers were left on board. The prize-crew, far too few to work the ship, found themselves drifting down on the coast of Trafalgar. They laboured to clear the wreckage off her deck, and fired her guns to request a tow, but nobody came to them. When it was clear she was going ashore, the French began to lend a hand, and between them they got up a jury mast on the stump of the mizzen, which carried a sail and gave them steerage way.

That night the French agreed on their plan and invited the three British officers into a cabin. A formal discussion took place, with Magon's secretary as interpreter. After the noble defence of their ship, the Frenchmen claimed, they had a right to expect the protection of the British fleet: the prize-crew had asked for a tow, but in vain. The French therefore considered themselves released from the obligations they had contracted by their surrender, and proposed to take the ship: the British would be well treated, if they did not resist.

In fact, they could not resist. There were three of them, and a dozen French officers in the cabin. Outside it there were sixty British seamen and upwards of five hundred able-bodied French. Besides the thing was common sense: whoever was in command, there were only two places they could go – either on to the rocks, or into the bay of Cadiz. They argued, and did it to some effect, for they made the French promise the prize-crew's freedom as soon as they reached a French or Spanish port. But with that, they had to be content. The decision was announced, and the French crew raised a shout of 'Vive l'Empereur!'

With the gale astern they drove towards Cadiz. The light-house was burning, but they only had one man on board who claimed to know the entrance. Rather than try it in the pitch dark and rain, they got a cable on their only remaining main anchor – for one had been shot away – and they let it go. At dawn they found they were on the edge of a rock, in the middle of the bay of Cadiz, and as the tide fell the stern began to strike on it. The houses of the town were hardly a mile away.

This was a helpless situation. During the day they were mortified to see the rescue fleet sail out, and then return with the two hulks they recaptured. They fired guns, and sent a boat to intercept the fleet. As each ship passed, close by them on its way to safety, they hoped and expected it would come to help them; but each sailed on unheeding into the harbour mouth. Only the *San Justo* came to an anchor outside. She offered a tow. But the lower deck of the *Algésiras* was still encumbered with debris and the capstan was damaged, and before they could clear it away to haul the anchor short, the *San Justo* made sail again and entered the port alone. And the rock was smashing the rudder, the water rising in the hold, guns had cast adrift and had to be resecured, which was always a highly dangerous operation, and the single anchor cable was visibly fraying.

In the following night they had almost every narrow escape a sailor could imagine. This was a night when the wind rose to a hurricane, and a wild sea was running in the bay. A ship they could not identify loomed through the darkness out of control, drove past them broadside at the length of a yardarm and vanished into the darkness again to crash on the shore to leeward. They dragged their anchor, but a momentary shift of wind took them clear of the rock. They grounded again on another. They jettisoned everything they could move. At dawn they found the anchor cable worn through to a single strand – and a boat from the shore informed them that several small vessels had come to them, carrying anchors, but all had been lost with all hands.

Again, all the next forenoon, they were left without help. Probably, everyone thought they were in a hopeless position, too dangerous to approach. Rather than face another night, in which the cable would certainly have parted, they made up their minds to take the risk of trying to get under way at high tide, in the hope they could cross the rock on which they had grounded. A Spanish schooner helped to haul the ship round to the starboard tack. The sails filled, the jury masts took the strain – and they could not break out the anchor, it was foul on the rocky bottom. As a final desperate measure, they cut it away. She drifted to leeward, but the rudder worked, she answered the helm and cleared the rock and came into sheltered water, where she ran aground again. Next day a boat laid an anchor for them and they hauled themselves clear. They deserved to survive.

That night, the night of Wednesday October 23rd, the wind and sea had been the worst so far, and in the morning Collingwood was forced to his hardest decision. At 8.30 he made the general signal: 'Prepare to quit and withdraw men from prizes after having destroyed or disabled them if time permits.' That was one of Popham's standard phrases, and he repeated it to several individual ships. At ten o'clock he made what seems a more ruthless general signal: 'Withdraw English, cut masts and anchors away from prizes.' Within the next few hours he made exceptions: to Neptune, 'Wear prizes cutting spritsail yards away and masts and sails overboard'; and to ships north of Britannia, 'Try to preserve prize nearest you, order one ship to tow.'

It was hard in many ways: first because these ships were regarded as the personal property of the fleet, which they had fairly won and would sell under Act of Parliament to the country; and secondly because it called for another prolonged feat of seamanship, from men already almost tired to death, to take off the thousands of men who were still on board the prizes. And there was even more in it than that: a victory without any prizes seemed hardly a victory at all. There would be nothing to show for it. Too soon, they had fancied themselves sailing into Spithead with the flower of the French and Spanish fleets. But with this order, in the eyes of the fleet, almost all of the glory and profit went out of Trafalgar.

Yet everyone knew the time had come: this was one decision for which nobody criticized Collingwood. They simply could not take the prizes out: British ships would be lost if they persisted. One duty therefore remained, to stop the enemy repossessing them. Collingwood was as deeply upset about it as anyone, but he found a puritanical comfort: 'Such a triumph as the whole would have been, coming into port in England, might have made us proud and presumptuous, and we ought to be content with that good fortune which Providence has thought sufficient.'

So it began: the ghastliest episode of Trafalgar. A good many of the British ships by then had anchored close inshore to save themselves, although no order to anchor had been given. Here, close to Cadiz, were the Orion, Leviathan and Ajax, and the Donegal, which had joined from Gibraltar; and they had also brought to anchor the *San Agustin, Monarca, Argonaute* and *Bahama*. They began on that Thursday afternoon to bring the men out of the prizes. But they were far apart, and in the vast rolling sea the journey from ship to ship was perilous. Many boats and many men were lost. On Thursday night the *Monarca* parted her cable and was seen at daylight driving ashore to be wrecked with hundreds of men still in her. Three days later British crews wore still at work to get men out of the others. In the end the *Argonaute* and *San Agustin* were scuttled. The *Berwick* was set on fire, and she drove ashore burning.

Out at sea, where prizes were still in tow, the work was more urgent; and again, of course, the wounded suffered most. Several ships combined to take off the huge crew of the *Santisima Trinidad*. 'What a sight,' a lieutenant of her prize-crew wrote, 'when we came to remove the wounded, of which there were between three and four hundred. We had to tie the poor mangled wretches round their waists, and lower them down into a tumbling boat, some without arms, others no legs, and lacerated all over in the most dreadful manner.' Who could tell, down in the darkness among three hundred dead, whether all the living were taken out before the ship was sunk? The Spaniards thought they were not. 'Up through the hatchways came a hideous shriek,' one Spanish account recalled. 'It came from the wretches on the lower deck, who already felt the water rising to drown them.'

They did their best, but many men were left in many ships, and after surviving the battle they drowned when the ships were scuttled, or died in the shipwrecks. Some British ships were packed with prisoners; in the Orion, which was a small ship, Codrington had his own crew of about five hundred, one hundred men from other British ships, and five hundred and eighty prisoners: the dirt, stench and confusion, he said, were almost intolerable.

On Sunday the 27th, six days after the battle, the storm slowly began to ease. Collingwood sent a boat into Cadiz, under a flag of truce. It took a letter from him to the Spanish Captain-General of the province, the Marquis de la Solana: he offered to send all the wounded prisoners ashore. It is not clear from any logs or journals who delivered the letter, but it was probably

Blackwood: he certainly went with another letter a few days later, into the harbour he had watched so long. All through the week of the battle and the storm, he had not taken off his clothes, but to visit the Spanish governor he put on a gold-laced cocked hat, a gold-laced coat and epaulettes, white pantaloons and hessian boots, a light crooked sabre, and a great shirt frill which was particularly fashionable. He was rowed in the barge he had recently painted, and accompanied by the midshipman Hercules Robinson, who had smelled the breeze off the land on that morning when they first saw the enemy's topsails hoisted. Blackwood's immaculate rig won admiration from the Spaniards in the streets, and the Marquis received him cordially with sherry and pineapple: the midshipman ate more than was polite. Collingwood's offer was gratefully accepted, and the Marquis offered in return to send out all the officers and men of the prize-crews who had been driven ashore. 'I can even add,' he said in his answering letter, 'that if your Excellency should need any assistance for your own wounded men, I shall deem it a pleasure and a duty to furnish it, and even to effect their cure upon land, if your Excellency will entrust them to me.'

The next day French frigates came out of the port flying flags of truce, and the exchange began. Survivors of the prize-crews came back with remarkable stories of the kindness they had met ashore: the Spaniards, they said, had done everything for them. Officers had been fêted. The master of the Orion had been on board the *Rayo* when she foundered, and a Spanish boat had taken him into Cadiz. As it approached the shore, a carriage was backed into the water so that he could step into it. Drinks and confectionery had been put in the carriage for him, and women and priests gave him all sorts of delicacies as it passed through the streets to a lodging where a bed with clean linen had been prepared. If he had been wrecked in England, he said, he would never have received one half the attention he did from the poor Spaniards, whose friends he had been destroying.

In those days naval war was fought with a graceful courtesy. Navies indeed, at any period of history, have usually fought with more mutual regard than armies: a sailor remains a sailor, whichever side he is on. Many British captains had their opponents as guests for two or three weeks, and found them agreeable companions. The pedantic and scholarly Codrington grew to like Infernet, the rumbustious captain he took from the *Intrepide*: he said he had delicacy in his conduct, although he was boisterous in his manner. Another captain in Gibraltar, who had not fought in the battle, insisted on giving Infernet a trunk with two dozen shirts, stockings, a bed, some cloth to make him a coat, and a draft for £100 – in token, he said, of the civility he had received when he had been a prisoner of the French navy. And Codrington, sending him at last to internment in England, wrote home to his wife. 'As his wife and family are at Toulon, and he has nothing but his pay, I wish you to supply any wants he may have to the amount of £100. I shall give him your address.'

And Collingwood, still off Cadiz, began a correspondence with the senior Spaniards which was full of compliments and formal expressions of regard and admiration. He inquired after the health of the wounded admirals, expressed his grief – and no doubt it was sincere – when Gravina died of wounds he received in the battle, and congratulated Alava, his opponent of the *Santa Ana*, on his recovery. And, in reply, they thanked him for his kindness, praised his skill, and commended some of the prize-crews to him for politeness and propriety. 'My Lord Marquis,' Collingwood wrote to the Captain-General in November, 'I beg your Lordship will accept my very best thanks for your kind present of a cask of most excellent wine. As a token of your esteem, it is peculiarly grateful to me. I wish I had anything half so good to send your Excellency: but, perhaps, an English cheese may be a rarity at Cadiz; and I accordingly take the liberty of begging your Lordship's acceptance of one, and of a cask of porter.'

The real sailors among the French and Spaniards had fought with courage, and had nothing to be ashamed of: on the contrary, as time passed they recollected individual deeds with national pride – those of Infernet, Churruca and Lucas were among them. But they accepted defeat without rancour, and the defeat was overwhelming. Dumanoir and his four ships were intercepted by four British ships on November 3rd, and all of them were captured. In Cadiz, the French had nothing left except their frigates and one line-of-battle ship, the *Neptune*, which was possibly fit for service. The Spaniards had a few more, but they never used them again. No doubt the humanity in victory, which Nelson prayed for and Collingwood exercised, confirmed the belief of many Spaniards that they were on the wrong side, and so encouraged them to throw off Napoleon's domination and open the way for Wellington in the Peninsular War. The victory did not lead to a peace, as Nelson had vainly hoped, but it did convince Napoleon of the truth his admirals had known and failed to tell him – that Britain could not be beaten on the sea.

The dismasted Belleisle was first to reach Gibraltar, on Thursday the 24th; the Naiad frigate, which had towed her there, cast her off in the harbour mouth and returned to duty. Already, the news of the battle had come through Spain, and she was greeted by a salute of guns. Boats towed her in, and as she passed, each ship in the harbour manned her yards and cheered. In the next ten days more ships crept in, their crews aware of each honourable scar. The Victory, towed by the Neptune, came to anchor on the evening of the 28th, with her flag at half mast.

People agreed that the storm had been far worse than the battle: indeed the battle already seemed a long time ago. Some sailors of lifelong experience said they had never seen such weather and certainly no sailing fleet was ever caught by a storm in such a dangerous situation. Yet every British ship survived it, and of the nineteen prizes they brought four in to Gibraltar. Nothing but years of training could have won that victory.

Safe, after their superhuman efforts, the captains in Gibraltar began to show weakness that was all too human: they bickered jealously. It was a reaction from danger, and from the bitter disappointment of the prizes, and from the sudden loss of Nelson's influence. Now they had no admiral at all, for Collingwood's sense of duty made him stay off Cadiz. 'Where our admiral is, God knows,' Codrington wrote to his wife as he stood towards the Strait, 'for none of us could find him all yesterday . . . This, surely, shows that the mind of a commander-in-chief should not be bent on trifles.' And Fremantle wrote to Betsey: 'The poor man does not know his own mind 5 minutes together.' They were jealous about the order in which they should go back to England: some, making light of their damage, had reported their ships fit for action; and these suspected that others, ordered to go home first, had exaggerated the repairs they needed. Some blamed Collingwood for not sending the whole fleet home together to make a triumphant arrival: Codrington said he was 'drivelling away the whole éclat of this glorious victory'.

And no doubt they argued about each other's part in the battle, for both these dissimilar men were annoyed by Captain Harvey of the Temeraire. Collingwood had especially mentioned the Temeraire in his dispatch – but this, the others said, was only because he had not seen any other captain before he wrote it. 'There will always be some whose vanity leads them,' Codrington wrote in his own pedantic style, 'to paint their conduct in too warm a tint, and to sound their own trumpets without regard to concord or harmony, but above all I have ever heard is Harvey . . . He is become the greatest bore I ever met with.' And Fremantle, more down to earth: 'Eliab Harvey goes with the next 5 ships, his head is turned, never having been in action before he thinks every Ship was subdued by him, and he wears us all to Death, with his incessant Jargon.' But Fremantle told his wife he was not dissatisfied: from prizes, he had captured himself an excellent French cook and a Spanish pug dog, the fatigue and employment had entirely driven away his bile – and in Gibraltar there were really some very pretty women.

The prize-money turned out better than they had feared, though not nearly so well as it would have if all the prizes had been saved. The four in Gibraltar were valued and the proceeds divided among the ships of the fleet; and, in addition, Parliament voted a special award of £300,000. In all, for the day's work, each captain received £3,362, and each seaman £6 10s.; and between these extremes, lieutenants and masters had £226, pursers, gunners, surgeons and masters' mates had £153, and such people as midshipmen, gunners' and bosuns' mates, clerks and sergeants of Marines had £37 each.

Collingwood's dispatch did include an unfair and prejudiced account of the Temeraire's action, which he undoubtedly heard from Captain Harvey. But otherwise it was an eloquent, modest and dignified report of what had happened – a literary achievement all the more astonishing because he wrote it in the cramped and heaving cabin of the Euryalus at the height of the storm. On the morning of Saturday the 26th he gave it to Lieutenant Lapenotiere of the Pickle schooner and sent him to England; and two days later he sent the Entreprenante cutter to Faro in Portugal with another copy, for the Ambassador in Lisbon to forward to the Admiralty. The Pickle with the gale behind her reached Falmouth in eight days. Lapenotiere landed and drove to London, 265 miles in thirty-seven hours. He arrived at the Admiralty at 1 a.m. on November 5th, a fortnight after the battle, and the First Lord was roused from his bed. A courier from Portugal is said to have come in a few minutes later. Early in the morning, the King was informed at Windsor and the news was officially published. Next day, *The Times* reported the general feeling: 'We know not whether we should mourn or rejoice. The country has gained the most splendid and decisive Victory that has ever graced the naval annals of England: but it has been dearly purchased. *The great and gallant NELSON is no more.*'

Next day it published the dispatch in full, and people read Collingwood's expression of his sorrow. 'My heart is rent with the most poignant grief for the loss of a friend, to whom, by many years of intimacy, and a perfect knowledge of the virtues of his mind, which inspired ideas superior to the common race of men, I was bound by the strongest ties of affection, – a grief, to which even the glorious occasion in which he fell does not bring the consolation which, perhaps, it ought.' His grief was reflected in London: 'There was not a man who did not think that the life of the Hero of the Nile was too great a price for the destruction of twenty sail of French and Spanish men of war . . . If ever there were a hero who merited the honour of a public funeral, it is the pious, the noble and the gallant NELSON, the darling of the British navy, whose death has plunged a whole nation into the deepest grief.' Illuminations were set up in the cities to celebrate the victory, but most of them were draped in black and purple. In provincial towns the news was read out by mayors, and *The Times* correspondent in Deal described the scene in these words: 'Instead of the air being rent with enthusiastic vociferations, and extravagant huzzas, a sullen gloom pervaded every countenance, and a dead silence for a time ensued, which at length terminated in a general ejaculation; when "Poor NELSON," with a faltering voice, and inarticulate sigh, was mournfully repeated by all that were present.' And a colleague in London observed with heavy humour that on the pavement in Whitehall 'a squadron of shattered tars were drawn up in *line of battle*, at anchor, with their lights *aloft*, all *well stowed* with *grog*, flourishing their mutilated stumps, *cheering all hands*, and making the best of their position, in collecting *prize-money*'.

Perhaps it can never exactly be true that a nation is plunged in grief. But it was undeniably true that the grief of Nelson's host of friends spread out, first to the fleet as a whole and then, in diminishing degrees, to people further and further removed from naval affairs. By the time the news of Trafalgar was known, it was common knowledge that Napoleon had withdrawn his army from Boulogne and the threat of invasion was in abeyance for the winter. Trafalgar brought assurance that the threat could never be renewed. Yet the death of Nelson undermined that feeling of security. In the minds of all classes of people, Nelson had personified the navy: they had felt it was

Nelson who protected them. Now it seemed that an era had ended; nobody could be sure that the navy without him could do what he had done, and continue to keep them safe.

After repairs in Gibraltar, the Victory sailed for England on November 2nd, in company with the Belleisle. Through adverse winds and her own decrepit state, the voyage took nearly five weeks. She put in to Spithead, but was ordered to proceed to Sheerness in the mouth of the Thames.

Beatty had hoped for instructions, and perhaps for profession-al consultation, about the body he still had in his care, but nobody came to the ship at Spithead to offer him any. On the contrary, he heard the body was to lie in state at Greenwich, exposed to the public. During ε long journey, he had twice drawn off the brandy from the cask and renewed it, but he was apprehensive about his experiment. On the way up Channel from Spithead, he therefore opened the cask and took the body out. Externally, he was relieved to find, it was still in perfect preservation. He made a complete autopsy, removing internal organs, and he also extracted the musket ball, and found the gold lace of Nelson's epaulette firmly embedded in it. He put the body in a lead coffin, which he filled with brandy, camphor and myrrh. On December 21st, off Sheerness, Nelson's own coffin was brought on board – the coffin made of the wood of the *Orient*, which he had been so pleased to be given after the Battle of the Nile; and to this the body was again transferred, in the presence of Hardy, the officers of the ship, and several of Nelson's friends. Dr. Scott, ever faithful, accompanied it in a yacht to Gravesend, and watched by it continuously during the two weeks it lay in state in the Painted Hall; and went with it again, escorted by hundreds of boats, up river to Westminster.

The funeral was the most splendid in living memory: royalty and nobility, ministers, admirals and generals led a procession so long that its head had reached St. Paul's before the end of it had started from Whitehall. Hardy and Blackwood carried emblems, and men of the Victory marched with the funeral car, but most of the captains of Trafalgar were still at sea, and no place in the ceremony had been allowed for Dr. Scott. At the last minute, left in Whitehall, he had to beg to be allowed to go in the carriage of some of Nelson's relations. 'Ah, poor fellow!' he said, with tears in his eyes, 'I remained with him as long as I could, and then they turned me away.'

Villeneuve was brought to England by Blackwood in the Euryalus, and he was interned at Reading. But in April he was freed and allowed to go back to France. In a hotel bedroom at Rennes he wrote a letter to his wife. 'How will you receive this blow? I weep more for you than myself. The fact is, I have reached a point where life is a disgrace and death a duty. Here, denounced by the Emperor, rejected by his minister who was my friend, charged with an immense responsibility in a disaster for which I am blamed and to which I was led by fate, I have to die. I ask your forgiveness for it, but it must be done, I am driven to it by the most violent despair . . . Adieu, adieu, comfort my family and those to whom I may be dear. I would have liked to end now, but I cannot. How lucky I have no child to receive my awful heritage and be burdened with my name! Ah, I was not born for such a fate, I never sought it, I have been forced to it despite myself. Adieu, adieu.'

This tragic and enigmatic letter was seized and suppressed by Napoleon's chief of police, and his wife was not told how he died. Later, officials said he was found with six knife-wounds, but Napoleon said he killed himself with a long pin, in order to avoid court martial. Some Frenchmen, then and ever since, have suspected he was assassinated. However it happened, his death was convenient. All the blame could be put on him. Long afterwards, the Emperor said the court martial would have shown he had disobeyed his orders: he had ordered him, he said, not to sail from Cadiz, and not to engage the English. Had he forgotten? Could even he have so deceived himself? Truth could be twisted and any man disgraced to preserve the myth of the Emperor's infallibility. But a just court martial, if justice had been possible, could not have condemned Villeneuve: it could only have placed the weight of the blame for Trafalgar on the Emperor himself.

INDEX